Choosing &
Changing

ALSO BY RICHARD GROSSMAN

Bold Voices

Richard
Grossman

Choosing
&
Changing

A Guide to
Self-Reliance

E. P. DUTTON · NEW YORK

For information contact:
E.P. Dutton, 2 Park Avenue,
New York, N.Y. 10016

Library of Congress Cataloging in Publication Data

Grossman, Richard L.
Choosing and changing.

Bibliography: p.
Includes index.
1.   Self-reliance.   2.   Choice (Psychology)
3.   Change (Psychology)   I.   Title.
BF723.S29G76   1978   158'.1   78-4073

ISBN: 0-525-07940-8

Published simultaneously in Canada by
Clarke, Irwin & Company Limited, Toronto and Vancouver

Designed by The Etheredges

10 9 8 7 6 5 4 3 2

For Ann

Contents

x · Contents

Choosing & Changing

1.
Who Am I?

Life and living are not the same: life is a capacity that is given to us; living is the process by which we use that capacity. The gift of life is supremely ironic. It is a gift of no specified height or depth, no predetermined breadth, and no predictable length. The dowry comes with a condition: the obligation to define the gift itself. We spend a life in the living of it.

We do not spend our lives alone. We are born of the living womb, released into the world of the living, and thrust into living our undefined lives alongside others. Life breathes in us; but it also surrounds us with masses of other breathing, active lives in pursuit of *their* definitions, of the boundaries of *their* gifts.

Living, in its larger definition, includes both the encounter with the outside world and the experience of events by our inner consciousness. Living is a process that flows constantly between these two poles of existence. Finding a balanced course between living in the world of physical and material needs and living in the world of our inner consciousness is an old dilemma. Too often, the weight is on the side of our physical and material circumstances. For many of us, the attempt at self-definition will coincide with an inventory of what we have—or, conversely, what we don't have. This point of view was described by William James when he wrote,

> It is clear that between what a man calls *me* and what he calls *mine* the line is difficult to draw. We feel and act about certain things that are ours very much as we feel and act about ourselves. Our fame, our children, the work of our hands, may be as dear to us as our bodies are, and arouse the same feelings and the same acts of reprisal if attacked . . . In its widest possible sense, however, a man's self is the sum total of all that he can call his, not only his body and his psychic powers, but his clothes and his house, his wife and children, his ancestors and friends, his reputation and works, his land and horses and yacht and bank account. All these things give him the same emotions. If they wax or prosper, he feels triumphant, if they dwindle and die away, he feels cast down—not necessarily in the same degree, but in much the same way for all.

But how true is this? It would appear that James—great psychologist though he was—looked on possessions as the extension of a healthy ego, and did not recognize that they might become chains binding down a constricted self. In our own day, more and more people are discovering with dismay that to hold on to what one has can easily turn out to mean being *held* by it. The self that wraps itself around what it possesses is, in a sense, trapped in its own past, blinded by that past to the possibilities of the present, and thus doubly cut off from the possibilities that lie ahead. Since possessions are necessarily ephemeral, the self becomes a kind of miser—a self haunted by concern with what is, in fact, already behind it.

The traits of a self thus haunted come in as many combinations as there are individuals. But certain bundles of those traits are common enough to be recognizable as types. To take a few examples, there are the Accumulator; the Cliffhanger; the Depression Baby; the Media Freak; the Cultist.

The ACCUMULATOR is frequently plump if not grossly overweight. His appetite for things extends to food, the more and richer the better, since the Accumulator tends to equate quantity with satisfaction. His closets fill up with clothes; new furniture is regularly added to the old; every new activity entails a multiplicity of uniforms and equipment. Such a person's pattern of living is circular and frenetic. You may hear him say, "I no sooner think I have it made than some new expense crops up, and I'm off and running. Every year my income goes up, and every year there's nothing left over but more debts!"

The Accumulator is not simply an exponent of conspicuous consumption; he is, more accurately, the ultimate consumer. His speech is peppered with elite brand names—Vuitton, Gucci, Adidas, Klipsch, and so on—but he is not so much "keeping up with the Joneses" as he is struggling to keep up with himself. He is not by nature a hoarding personality; he has simply committed his energy and attention to material objects that then become his masters.

Thus when he speaks of his life, the Accumulator can talk only about its physical aspects: the state of his health, his property, and whatever issues bear directly on it. Politics for him is tax loopholes and depreciation; crime is the increased threat to his property; marriage is an enterprise of which he is president and his wife a sort of executive vice president or chief of staff. At his most extreme, the Accumulator is a person without a center. An inner self is the one luxury in which he will not indulge, since all around him are the proofs of his existence and the reasons for its continuation.

The CLIFFHANGER embodies a subtler form of the confusion between "me" and "mine." He is likely to be thin—not only because he eats less than others, but because he burns up calories in worrying. His big stake is in being regarded as a successful juggler and negotiator with his many creditors. He will spend hours in calculating what he has and does not have: monthly income and outgo, calendars of payments and receipts, and installment plans that are being continually revised. He is always looking for new ways to spread his resources in the effort to unburden himself of his perennial indebtedness. But all the while he is slipping deeper into "hock," as he calls it, because he cannot keep up with his own schemes for getting free of obligation.

The Cliffhanger has *become* his struggle.

Whether the struggle is one originally imposed by a selfless effort to help someone else, or simply the result of his own poor management, the result for the Cliffhanger is the same. He is under a constant strain, putting off the oil company here and the credit company there, and so on, until he exhausts his physical strength, losing the appetite for sex and the ability to relax. Sensitive as he is to what he lacks, he tends to become a crabbed personality— wanting not to leave the house because things "out there" cost money, unwilling to meet new people because that may entail amusements that he cannot spare the time for, even if he could afford them. With old friends he maintains the façade of endurance: "Sure, we're broke, but we can get along until I get things straightened out." In his own eyes, bearing up under the burden of debt makes him heroic; courting bankruptcy, he feels like an adventurer. Trapped in his own history, the Cliffhanger has invested his whole identity in his own ceaseless, scrambling struggle to become solvent.

The DEPRESSION BABY does not necessarily speak of being haunted by the thought of breadlines, soup kitchens, and once-wealthy men reduced to selling apples. But the specter of living through another Great Depression is apparently not limited to those of us who were children during the Thirties. We see all around us, often in men and women too young to have had any such experience, those whose devotion to gaining material security for themselves and their children comes to dominate their lives. They throw themselves into work with the voraciousness of an addict. Since they need to see the direct result of their efforts, they are especially good at concrete tasks, and have little patience with art, music, or sports as a recreation—luxuries indulged in by an invisible elite to which no true worker could ever belong. Their sense of reality is confirmed by the promise of a hard job waiting for them every morning, something they can get their teeth into. The reply given by Clarence Darrow, the noted trial attorney, to the question of what he considered the secret of the good life, fits the Depression Baby perfectly: "You go from one hard job to another—and then you're just about as well off as when you're dead."

The Depression Baby has no truck with the concept of an inner self. He is, after all, most himself when he is overloaded with work and responsibility. As an addictive worker he may indeed accumulate both money and power; but these are secondary considerations. Only work, and the assurance that he will always be able to work, persuades him that he is indeed alive.

The MEDIA FREAK wants the latest information immediately, before it can cool and be superseded. He picks up and as promptly drops names, events, precise figures. He must always be abreast of the latest developments. As fitful and restless as the diet on which he feeds, he sleeps lightly, eats too fast, moves rapidly, and is usually looking over your shoulder as he speaks to you, ever alert for the arrival of the latest thing on his horizon. He is the ultimate extension of David Riesman's "inside-dopester." For the Media Freak, "peer-group satisfaction" has become addictive; he needs an audience every minute, surviving within the world where he is worker, friend or parent by being a performer even there. St. Paul might have been describing him when he wrote that "all the Athenians and strangers which were there spent their time in nothing else, but either to tell, or to hear some new thing."

As a result of all this, the Media Freak's personal nature succumbs to atrophy. His inner consciousness is haunted, having been taken over by a commodity whose value is in being ephemeral, by the acquisition of what does not endure.

The CULTIST thinks of himself as a student. Last year he was taking Kendo lessons; this year he is going to master the one hundred twenty-eight positions of what he thinks is T'ai Chi Chuan. He has also bought into a lot of other things: Royal Canadian Air Force exercises, jogging, long-distance running, Aikido, weightlifting, Hatha Yoga—all sorts of disciplines entailing a manual, a course, a workshop. "None of these things is the whole answer—I know that," he will tell you. "But the more I get in touch with my body [or mind, or feelings] the better I am as a person. You've got to work at these things, really learn how to use your body [or mind, or feelings]."

In pursuit of that learning how, a system or a teacher is the focus. The Cultist has new experiences, some of which are deceptively transforming. He does learn new ways to move or eat or breathe or concentrate. Why, then, is he forever moving from one system to another? How many courses must he take before he can move on to applying what he has learned to simply getting on with the job of living?

The reason would appear to be that the Cultist is trying to get answers without having formulated the one important question. Because the teacher seems to have his act together, to be centered or peaceful or integrated, the Cultist believes he can be likewise by doing what the teacher does. So the question becomes, "Am I doing it right?"—not "Why am I doing it at all?" Until he asks the latter question, he has not consulted his own deepest needs, not taken a look into the nature of his particular destiny. He wants take-home salvation, convenience-food meditation, six-pack sex, spray-can assertiveness and power. He wants the whole shopping cart filled, and he is willing to pay for it.

Most of what is picked up at the consciousness take-out counter will not hurt anyone. Some of it may become part of the regular diet, but with no great effect. So the Cultist keeps going back for new products, new techniques, new systems. Yet none of these psycho-hypodermics seem to last. After the Arica fix he had to have *est;* when that wore off, he found he needed Assertiveness Training to handle the kids, and then came the Man–Woman Thing workshop. He has been misled into supposing that a subscription to the guru-of-the-month can lead to enlightenment. In accepting such packaged substitutes, he has stopped relying on himself. And thus he falls victim to the same feelings of emptiness that haunts the Accumulator, the Cliffhanger, the Depression Baby, and the Media Freak.

In one way or another, each of these types has failed to draw a clear line between *being* and *having*. In those moments when emptiness threatens, in realizing the bankruptcy of their attachments, they experience the terror of the question: *Who am I?*

To ask this question is not to have arrived at a dead end. On the contrary, it can be the signal of a new beginning. Or the signal may take the form of a question that at first appears commonplace: "Isn't there someplace I could move to where I could meet some new people?" or "Will I ever find the time to write?" In the wistfulness of such question we can recognize, if we try, something more than boredom or complaining. The seeker after new friends is saying, "I haven't found my community, the people I can really share things with." The frustrated writer is saying, "I really could create something beautiful or funny or original."

The signal can be heard as well in more acute forms of distress. Men and women who identify themselves as being in a "career crisis" are likely to exclaim, "I never thought I'd end up just . . ." A wise clergyman once told me that among couples who came to him for his help as a marriage counselor, the signal of the deepest misery came from those who admitted that *nothing was happening* between the two of them.

The signal of distress may manifest itself in the alienation, depression, and *accidie* that characterize so many—or simply in the guilty knowledge that one is not being one's best self. The psychoanalyst Medard Boss writes of this condition: "If you lock up potentialities, you are guilty against (or *indebted* to) what is given you in your origin, in your 'core.' In this existential condition of being indebted and being guilty are founded all guilt feelings, in whatever thousand and one concrete forms and malformations they may appear in actuality."

William James wrote of this same failure: "I have no doubt whatever that most people live, whether physically, intellectually, or morally, in a very restricted circle of their potential being. They *make use* of a very small portion of their possible consciousness and of their soul's resources in general, much like a man who, out of his whole bodily organism, should get into the habit of using and moving only his little finger."

It need not be so. This book reflects the belief expressed by Ralph Waldo Emerson, that "nothing can give you peace but yourself," and its corollary, that "all men have my blood, and I all men's." Convinced that healthy societies grow from healthy individuals, and vice versa, I offer a map drawn by an optimist. The territory to be covered is the whole of adult life—that vast area that extends from our inner consciousness to the world outside of us, and in which we travel through events with other people. My optimism is not about the terrain itself—a strange and unpredictable landscape certainly—but about those who are in the process of traversing it. I am convinced that the reports of quicksands and dragons to be found there have been greatly exaggerated. I do not believe it is only saints and heroes who get through successfully.

My optimism stems from observing how wonderfully equipped quite ordinary people are for the journey. The healthiest people I know are characterized by loving the task of making their own lives. They see obstacles and disappointments not as something to "get over" or to be gotten past, but rather as something to *go through.* These people do not see life as an enemy to be confronted and conquered. Their concern is with going forward, toward goals they have set out of a knowledge of their own natures—knowledge gained both through experience and through introspection.

I would not suggest that such healthy people never make mistakes, never become depressed, cause injury to others, or lose their sense of direction. What shows their health is that they are able to accept those events, too—understanding that they are not infallible, that they will doubtless falter from time to time. Their resilience springs from a belief that the process of living is more important than "getting there." They relish discovering themselves in ways they have come to understand are uniquely right for them. They may never be perfectly balanced, but they are always engaged in balancing; the opposing forces in a healthy nature may never be perfectly harmonized, but are always harmonizing; they may never become perfectly autonomous, but they are always moving toward self-reliance.

For healthy people, means are as important as

ends; they can immerse themselves in work or love or play for the sake of doing work, being in love, frolicking at play. They delight in their experiences, and they feel lucky to have consciousness and choice, to be able to choose what they do and be awake to that choosing. Such people are truly prosperous, not in the everyday sense of having accumulated goods and wealth, but in the original meaning of the word: thriving, flourishing, vividly themselves.

Moving toward this personal prosperity begins with the courage to *ask the big questions* about ourselves: Can I make a difference in the world? What is my true destiny, my vocation? How can I reconcile my own sense of vocation with the demands of the world around me? Can I trust my own urges? Can I really change the direction of my life?

We have traditionally left questions like these to artists, philosophers, and poets. We have left it to the poets to paint "the inner visions of the heart," to philosophers to examine the meaning of those visions, to scientists to expand them into material form. It is time to reclaim that agenda for ourselves.

2.
Our Many Selves

If we are to ask the big questions, we must begin by opening the way for them to be asked—which means finding a new means of translating the language of small doubts in which they are so often heard at first. Here, as in much of this book, I have gone back to the thinking of Emerson, who wrote in his essay entitled *Fate:*

> One key, one solution to the mysteries of the human condition, one solution to the old knots of fate, freedom and foreknowledge exists: the propounding, namely, of the double consciousness. A man must ride alternately on the horses of his private and public nature, as the equestrians in the circus throw themselves from horse to horse, or plant one foot on

the back of one and the other foot on the back of the other.

Here, as usual, Emerson makes uncommonly good sense. The two levels of living are surely recognizable to anyone. There is my public nature —the one who goes off to work; who says "Good morning" to the bus driver; who is greeted as "Mr. Grossman" by the new receptionist at the office; who signs a letter, in my neatly defined role as "Director," to someone in London whom I've never met; who orders a tunafish salad plate at lunch; who talks on the phone with an insurance broker about premiums; who pauses in the corridor to speak with a new staff member—in short, the part of my nature that goes about its business in the world of public doings, playing the roles of commuter, employer, project director, customer, and colleague.

When I get back to the intimacy of home, I slip into my private nature—the relaxed, unbuttoned self who hugs my wife and pets the cat as I come in; who phones my daughter to find out what the eye doctor had to say; who mends the veneer on the dining-room table; who compares notes with friends on a movie we've all just seen—who, with a somewhat altered set of manners, goes about playing another set of roles, as husband, father, householder, and personal friend.

Emerson saw clearly that the healthy life is made up of both kinds of experience, committing us to behave in different ways as we shift from one role to another. He seems to be urging balance as we make that shift. But however clear all this may be, there remains a question: If the two aspects of this double-mounted, equestrian existence are indeed aspects of one and the same self, what is it that makes that self one? What motive power, what animating center, governs the shift from the private to the public role, and back again?

Considering this question, we recognize a third aspect—the "I" who sees myself in both roles, who has chosen how they are to be filled. There is, in other words, an island of consciousness that is identified wholly with no single role, that recognizes no name but "I"—that center which exists *both before and after* the role is played, the point of anchorage for both the public and the private selves. Taking Emerson's image of the two aspects of consciousness as a point of departure, I see human personality as made up of three layers:

The *public* nature: those aspects that become visible in the roles you play as a member of society.

The *private* nature: the parts of yourself that come into play in your most intimate encounters with family and close friends.

The *personal* nature: the inner core of the consciousness, which observes and directs your outward behavior, and that is the true source of your own individual destiny.

Such an anatomy of personality permits us to think of ourselves in new ways. Learning more about how our public, private, and personal selves are interconnected can help us to see what is unique about us. It will show us how to merge our special values and goals with our obligations to other people. Above all, it will enable us to define the vocation that is the heart of true prosperity. The familiarity we gain with our many selves will lead to a new confidence that we can be the persons we were meant to be—more authentically ourselves.

The relations among the public, the private, and the personal natures can be thought of as something like what happens to a rubber ball in motion. As a ball bounces, its surface strikes against other surfaces, hitting the floor or the walls, and also striking against other balls so that they bounce, too. Underneath the outer layer of each ball—which we can envision as representing the public self—is a layer that absorbs the vibrations from the outer surface, though it does not strike them directly: this is the private nature. Still deeper, at the center of each sphere, isolated from the random events that are going on outside it, is the core—the "I" that is central to each human personality. Here our analogy breaks down, for the reason that unlike a rubber ball—unlike any inanimate object—the outer sphere in a human being is *controlled at the core.* The human personality is self-directing, self-propelling, self-governing—all qualities deriving from the ability and the obligation to choose. José Ortega y Gasset described the obligation in this way: "At every moment of the day I must decide what I am going to do in the next moment; and no one can make that decision for me, or take my place in this. . . . In the final analysis, each one of us carries his existence suspended in the hollow of his hand."

To visualize this process in action, we can imagine a man going to a doctor for a routine checkup. At the conclusion of the examination his physician tells him that his blood pressure is up, and that something will have to be done. Reminding him that hypertension makes him susceptible to the threat of heart disease or stroke, among other problems, the physician may suggest to his patient that although high blood pressure is a specific physical symptom, it may be related to other, nonphysical circumstances such as stress or worry. He may suggest finding ways to "relax a little more," or urge him "not to take things quite so seriously," concluding the session with advice about diet and a prescription for a drug to ease his condition.

In the usual nature of things, the encounter between physician and patient takes place entirely at the level of the public nature—notwithstanding the private concerns that are implicit for the patient. When he goes home, of course, the condition takes on another dimension. At the dinner table, when he tells his wife and family that his blood pressure is up —"nothing to worry about, I just have to be a little careful and take some pills"—the whole family becomes involved. The children may want to know, for example, whether he can still go on the backpacking trip that has been scheduled. After they have left the table, the man and his wife may go on to talk about the "other factors" the doctor has mentioned—the problems at work, the worry about having enough money for everything they have planned. The entire climate of the family's life will have been subtly altered by the unspoken threat he has brought home to them. This is the world where the *private* nature functions.

Later that night, with his wife asleep beside him, the man will find himself alone with the meaning of the day's events. He now inhabits an island—the "I" at the core of his entire consciousness. Aware that he alone can choose how to act in response to the conditions that surround him, and in particular those of his physical body, he comes face to face with the big, fundamental questions: What do I do now? What are my priorities? Where do I start from? He is now conscious at the deepest level of his being, alive at a point from which he views the workings of his public and private natures, but deeper than either.

How does this personal nature, this "I," reveal itself in us?

To help in answering the question, try turning the question, *Who Am I?,* into an exercise. Begin by making a list of every aspect of yourself that you can think of. Take plenty of time; write down each item as a complete sentence: "I am a man"; "I am an accountant"; and so on. If you are like most people who have done this exercise, you will probably have begun by listing your gender, your job, your religion, your status as spouse, parent, and member of an extended family. After listing such obvious social and private roles, you will have gone on to the labels others use to describe you. Then you will probably have listed certain traits you consider especially applicable: "I am impatient"; "I am hardworking"; "I am musical." Then, perhaps, you will have put down some secret ways in which you think of yourself: "I am a bird"; "I am royal"; "I am a stream." Finally, you may have set down some identification of yourself with the universe: "I am all men"; "I am the heavens."

Such an exercise can demonstrate not merely the ability to imagine and articulate, but above all the *awareness* that lies within the personal nature—awareness of itself and of the world that lies outside. The "I" at the center of the personal nature, in seeing itself, is at the same time aware of options; it experiences the power of being free to choose. It is this "I" who watches as I carry on all my public and private roles. It is this "I" who chooses to fill those roles, to be known as the one who fills them. It is the homebone, the heart of our existence. Here we exist *before* we enact our own particular life dramas. It is in this center that our public and private selves are anchored—the naked and unassailable core of consciousness from which each one of us moves out into the world, and to which each one of us retreats when we have done with that world—or when it appears to have done with us.

This personal nature is as unique to each of us as a thumbprint. However much we may share in universal human traits and dispositions, however much we are involved in *specieshood,* there are also the distinguishing, idiosyncratic traits that make up our *personhood.* It is these uncommon traits that fuse to become the personal nature, the ultimate governor of the public and the private selves.

Having identified what is unique to us—and in

us—we are better equipped to hear, and to *respect,* the demands of the personal nature. We may wonder whether the pressures from the personal self will be egocentric or self-aggrandizing—in other words, totally self-ish. Almost every time, however, the fear of heeding our own deeply personal urges will turn out to be a reflection of other voices and other judgments, especially the injunctions of parents: "You mustn't think of yourself all the time, dear"; "Don't make so much noise," or "Hush, your father's talking"; "Yes, but will it pay the rent?"; "When are you going to settle down?" The message of all such injunctions adds up to the reiteration that you can't always have what you want. There is, of course, truth in these echoed litanies. As children, especially as very young children, we needed to learn from the restraining voices of our parents. But as independent adults, we have learned only too well that it is impossible to think only of ourselves, that we cannot always have what we want when we want it. The world will have seen to that. There is still a grand distinction to be made between mere selfishness and the personal quest for meaning—and we must learn how to make it.

We must begin by acknowledging that the wishes of the personal nature are indeed not always entirely admirable, or pleasant to own up to. Indeed, according to the theories of human nature that have come down to us, as codified by religion and psychoanalysis, we are either doomed or damned: doomed to inherit the original sin of Adam and Eve, and thus condemned to lives of repentance that promise salvation only *after* this life; or damned to the bestiality our species is said to have "risen" from. According to the latter view, our animalism is held in uneasy check somewhere in the darker recesses of our unconscious, our only hope being that if we face the caged monsters (i.e., arrive at "insights" into our "repressions"), their awesome energy can be rechanneled into civilized pursuits (i.e., we can "sublimate" our basic "drives" and "instincts").

But we should remember that Freud's explorations were in the tradition of medical pathology; their focus was on discovering the sources of distress and disease, with the goal of restoring sick patients to a functioning state of health. What the Freudian vision, useful though it may be, does not concentrate on is what concerns us here: the use of conscious insight to go beyond *adequate* functioning to thriving, creative health—the exploration of what Abraham Maslow has called "the farther reaches of human nature."

Knowing that perfect self-realization is impossible, we need to go on listening for the sound, often no more than a whisper, of what Maslow called the "inner impulse voices." Often they come when we have had a glimpse of the power of our personal natures, when we have had the experience of being the right person in the right place at the right time, doing the right thing. On such occasions, we go into a kind of "overdrive," acting vigorously at a level above our usual performance, a kind of transcendent functioning. The tingle of excitement, the feeling of perfect attunement between ourselves and the world we inhabit, remains a source of wonder. At such moments the personality is like an orchestra. What we call "I" in our deepest moments of consciousness is the conductor; his reading of the score is our *awareness;* his baton is our *will.*

We are endowed with the energy to choose the direction into which our strength and power might go. In the words of Pico della Mirandola, "You may, as the free and proud shaper of your own being, fashion yourself in the form you may prefer. It will be in your power to descend to the lower, brutish forms of life; you will be able through your own decision to rise again to the superior orders whose life is divine."

It is the public nature that performs; the private nature that interacts; and the personal nature that *is* —is the organizer and conductor of the tendencies, skills, needs, values, and powers whose unique configuration defines us as living individuals.

3.
You Are
as You Choose

Equipped with a clearer vision of how our personalities are constructed, we can become more conscious of how we choose—or refuse to do so. The power to choose is the creative component of the personality —the option of committing ourselves to this person and not that one, to that job instead of the other, to act or to be at rest, to share our feelings or withhold them. The making of choices in the public and the private sphere is a skill that can improve as we acquire a deeper understanding of our own personal center. The ability to make choices that truly reflect our personal values is indeed our one resource for confronting the pressures to which we are subject. As we learn to distinguish among these pressures, we can learn to bring harmony out of our conflicts, and to deal with crisis as an opportunity for growth.

We make decisions as we choose among alternatives presented by the world around us, *and* as an expression of the intrinsic need to be ourselves. Such commonplace options as deciding what to order in a restaurant, what clothes to put on in the morning, what station to tune in on for the news, are in the nature of *selections.* They may be important, however mundane or transient; but they are made in a way quite different from those that come from within and that function as a creative expression of the personal nature.

Our public and private selves, navigating through a world of day-to-day complexities, often make such selections without any conscious process of choosing. Some, like the cluster of little choices we make in riding a bicycle or driving a car, are literally *un*conscious. Much of what we think of as our education is of this order: learning the sequential steps in a process trained through repetition and practice. If the process becomes habitual, we put sugar in our coffee without thinking, in much the way we step over cracks in the sidewalk, until there is a danger of becoming almost totally the creatures of the automatic response. The power of much advertising and propaganda lies in the encouragement of such unthinking selections. There is no doubt that we *can* be conditioned, manipulated, even finally deprived of any conscious choosing. But succumbing to the habit through conditioning *did* begin with an act of choice: we did choose to submit rather than to resist the process. It is all too easy to refer choice to others; and since taking responsibility is harder than giving it away, the habit of unconscious selection *could* turn us into a race of automatons, of binary reactors and mechanical echo chambers.

Expanded personal consciousness—the power to see what the choices are and act accordingly—can change that course. This means more than simply obeying what our parents so often cautioned, to "think before you act." In order to make fully conscious choices, we must refer back to our own values, and see choice-making as an active component of our own identity.

It is relatively simple to identify a meaningful decision when it involves our children, for example. *Selecting* a pair of shoes is clearly not of the same order as *choosing* a nursery school. But there are also choices that might appear "meaningless," but which, if examined thoughtfully, reveal themselves to have real importance. Suppose you agree, for example, to play one more set of tennis when you're already overtired. If the strain leads to a pulled muscle, you may be led to reexamine that "meaningless" decision. Did you play that extra set in order not to disappoint a partner, or because it seemed better to go along than admit to being tired? We need to become aware of how the part of our private or public selves that craves approval tends to yield to fashion or the apparent consensus. At such times the personal self that is to be a consistent arbiter of choice must not be dozing, but vigorously awake. For the personal self is the final authority where there is a conflict between rival pressures or needs. The "I" that makes the decision must be truly a voice from the center, not a half-conscious reflex that takes its cue from the outer layers of the personality. The next time you are too tired to play more tennis, will the personal self be in charge?

A good way of learning about how we make decisions is to keep a record of our experiences in choosing, through keeping a journal or workbook. Set aside a regular period of time each day, for at least a week, to examine your decision-making. Write down every instance you can recall of what and how you chose. Which choices were automatic (brushing your teeth, pouring a second cup of coffee)? Which were unconscious (lifting the garage door, lighting a cigarette)?

Then consider the more conscious and personal choices you have made. Review the sequence of your own behavior as if it were a slowed-down motion picture, to isolate the stopped frames where you made choices. Note the small, coping decisions: to continue or halt a conversation; to leave or stay at a dinner table; to hail a taxi or wait for the bus. Note the decisions made as matters of principle: to tell your husband he has hurt your feelings; to ask for a change of assignment rather than put up with your discontent any longer; to write a letter telling your son you miss him, and wish he would call. We all know, when we choose to know it, which are the choices that really come out of the personal nature. Such choices have meaning not simply because marriage, jobs, and parenthood have been widely identified as major concerns, but because of their particular relation to our own most precious and intimate values. Since those values become visible to us through our feelings, a review of this kind is helpful in developing a reliable sense of self—of *personality* as Carl Jung described it, "a definitely formed, psychic* abundance, capable of resistance and endowed with energy."

Keeping a journal will show what your real priorities are, but only so long as you keep an honest record. This means that any tendency toward disapproval or passing judgment from the outside must not be allowed to take over as you describe your choices. The purpose of recording your experience is to make it possible for you to revise the pattern of choice-making, not to punish yourself for failure. The "I" that acts is also the "I" that keeps the record, and there will be changes only when that same "I," having willed them, brings them about through conscious choice, through the countermanding mediation of your personal self. As Michael Polyani reminds us in his book *Personal Knowledge,* "The freedom of the subjective person to do as he pleases is overruled by the freedom of the responsible person to do as he must." If by keeping a personal journal we can begin to see how often we register a vote against our own possibilities by blaming some past inadequacy, we can also begin to uncover the positive urges that lie behind what so far we have only "dreamed" of doing. A journal can be the revealing chronicle of

*Meaning, of course, "of the psyche," not occult or mystical.

how we contend, or fail to contend, with inner negativism. Some of our negative stands may be genuine commitments, arrived at after much thought and experience—expressions of our personal values, and thus quite as authentic as the affirmative choices we make because we must.

Not choosing, of course, is in itself a choice, and entails its own peculiar consequences. Suppose, for instance, that you have been given an assignment at work, which you put off doing. The inner message counseling postponement is not usually direct; you simply find yourself reorganizing the top of your desk or sorting papers instead. Distractions by the dozen are available if we choose to find them. Much of this goes on without your noticing—or does it? Doesn't some part of you always know when you're stalling or procrastinating? Don't we usually acknowledge the postponement by going down a list of reasons for putting off what must be done? What we usually do *not* do is take the step beyond rationalizing, to get at the real reason why we're in this bind.

To get at that reason, it's time to sit back and have an honest conversation with yourself. It might go something like this:

"Who is fiddling around with that stack of papers?"

"I am."

"Which part of you?"

"Why, I guess the private me."

"Not the public one?"

"Well, maybe that one too."

"And what is the personal you doing?"

"Nothing."

"Nothing at all?"

"Well, nothing right now except rearranging these papers."

"And who is it who's not doing the report?"

"I'm the one."

"Which *you* do you mean?"

By some such process it begins to be clear that you—the personal you—has chosen not to do the report, in favor of something that either can wait or doesn't need doing anyhow. There will be a sense of relief when you make this honest statement, when you can see yourself not as a rotten, no-good procrastinator, but as having simply made a choice—one you are thus quite able to countermand at any time. The key to this examination is the respect it accords to your personal nature for the power to choose, even when the choice is one as unproductive as avoiding getting down to work. The obverse now becomes clear: your personal nature is just as capable of choosing—at *any* time—to do the work that has been assigned. The interior dialogue has unmistakably identified that capability.

Habit, enculturation, and circumstances all tend to combine to obscure the true role of the personal nature. In becoming aware of that role, we begin to see how often we confuse our lives with our circumstances. We resent and bemoan those circumstances when they are unfavorable, seeing ourselves as prisoners of misfortune. Honest introspection will often reveal, however, that what we complain of is the result of choices made *not* from the center of the personal nature, but as a reaction to stimuli from outside it.

Only as we listen to and make room for the personal nature to have its say will the degree to which we tend to abdicate be revealed even in the conventional aspects of our behavior. For example, instead of saying, "No thanks, I'd rather be alone on Saturday," we avoid owning up to ourselves with something like, "Oh, I'm terribly sorry, but Sam's uncle may be in town, and I just don't think we should make any plans. Suppose I call you on Friday . . ."

Avoiding small truths or facing large ones are both parts of knowing and respecting the urges of our personal natures. Yet knowledge and respect do not lead to authentic behavior unless they are accompanied by *trust*, by the belief that we can be responsible for the success or failure of our actions.

We can trust the newly discovered, or uncovered material residing deep in our personal centers because none of it can become behavior unless we *will* it to be so. The substance of personal inclination is raw ore mined by the exploring power of our awareness. It must be refined and annealed by the furnace of the will before it can become visible; and the "I" at the center of the personal nature can choose to use that refining power—or not.

4.
The Cost
of Not Choosing

What keeps us from choosing for ourselves? We can recognize a variety of largely irrational reasons: the notion that we're not entitled to have what we want; the fear that our choice may turn out to be the wrong one; the memory of previous failures. Almost always these blocks to free choice are anachronistic distortions of authority. Our parents' disapproval is not relevant to an adult decision, nor are the frustrations and disappointments of childhood. When we haul these memories up to the light of our conscious reason and see them for what they are, they become easier to dismiss and be free of.

Help in achieving a clearer perspective is the goal of psychotherapy. We are urged not to deny old fears, not to shrink from the pain of old experiences. The technique of uncovering and confronting such blocks is effective in dealing with our past experience. But other, no less subtle blocks to free and creative choosing are more difficult to deal with, because they have the appearance of being *legitimate.* Some of these also come from the past—not the past of unfaced or unresolved hurts but the active, remembered, statistical past that we invoke whenever we deal with our own biographies. This "active" past is the cumulative and crystallized memoir of ourselves that we present as "the way we've always been."

Many of us use this conscious past as an anchor or "security blanket." We feel the need for something solid and familiar to hold onto, and our own past experience is the one thing we can be certain of. At each point of contemplating ourselves, we are our past, our present, and our future. But the past is the only *known* quantity. If the present—or the prospect of the future—appears to include risk, we can retreat to the certainty of what has already happened. Suppose a child offers to share his crayons, inviting you to draw a picture—and you protest, "Oh, but I never could draw a straight line." For many people there is a whole litany of "I-never-coulds." "I never could carry a tune"; "I never could dance"; "I never could do math." Let it be acknowledged quickly that not everyone has to want to draw, or sing, or learn to dance. Free choosing always entails the option of refusal. "I never could stand to watch a bullfight" is not necessarily a mask of cowardice. Yet an important clue may lurk in the habit of invoking such refusals. We may be making the past into an obstruction, using it as a means of evading the present and thus the possibilities of the future. When you hear yourself complaining that these are "bad times," you may need to pause and ask whether you are doing anything to prevent yourself from acting to make them better.

"I never could get up and speak," or "I never could do anything in front of an audience" may turn out to be an example of abdication by the personal "I." This refusal may be legitimate, all the more since we live in a society where public appearances and performing before an audience bring such general approval. Being one's true self may mean standing with what looks like a minority, and declining to be a public performer of any kind. But here, as with everything else, the choice must be tested for *personal* validity. The only way to prevent the isolation of standing with the minority from becoming lonely is to be at home within the personal self. If we never question what we do in the name of the past, we are sure never to grow beyond it.

No less omnipresent, for some of us, is the authority of the Olympian "they." "They say"; "they're not wearing"; or, "they're not doing anything about crime"; "they're ruining the cities"; and so on and on. For adults this "they"—the unnamed authority—becomes the equivalent of the juvenile peer group. When we are young, venturing beyond the sanctuary of the family, the last thing we want is to be singled out as different. To be admitted into the group, to be one of "them," is the only comfortable way of moving from the known world into the unknown. Although we want more than anything to be differentiated from our families, we are not ready to be differentiated from our friends. So, for each generation, clothes, hair styles, slang catchwords, dance steps, music, and opinions are legislated into badges of respectability. (Ironically, most parents seem to have forgotten how *they* joined the crowd, and to become exasperated with their children as they join theirs.)

Just as irrational, and more depressing, is the degree to which "they" still hold sway over so many of us in adulthood. Ortega y Gasset has described this way of allowing ourselves to be taken over: "When I live on what they say, and fill my life with it, I have replaced the I which I myself am in solitude, with the mass 'I'—I have made myself 'people.' Instead of living my own life, I am *de*-living it by changing it to otherness." Operating on the premise that our life must be filled by others means allowing "them" to become situated at the center of our own being. Those of us who carry into adulthood the safety-oriented reflexes of a dependent childhood end up waiting for "them" to act and speak for us. Having abdicated acting for ourselves, we hang around waiting for "things to happen." For whatever then does happen, we then lay the entire responsibility at "their" door.

We have coined some subtle linguistic variations of this "them." We speak of how difficult it is for "one" to change jobs; or we may say, "You hardly dare walk the streets any more." Though the usage is correct, such locutions may also be a sign of displacement—personal experience has been assigned to an impersonal other. These seemingly trivial dodges have given rise to one of the ground rules of Gestalt therapy, the injunction to "own your own statement." In most Gestalt exercises participants agree not to use the second or third person in anything they say, on the premise that to do so is a way of avoiding responsibility ("ownership") for their own feelings and opinions. When we say, "You hardly dare walk the streets any more," what we really mean, of course, is that *we* are afraid. The second- or third-person construction is a way of deflecting our own fear. Ideas and feelings must be attributed to someone; but we disown them, putting them on the shoulders of an agent: "you," "one," or "them."

Minor? Negligible? Before thus dismissing today's seemingly trivial, half-conscious habit, we do well to consider whether today's half-conscious usage is on the way to becoming tomorrow's fixed reality. Little by little, such small usages can build up into a mesh of otherness. The merit of the Gestalt exercise is that it causes us, however artificially, to become conscious of the self at the center of our behavior, reminding us of how continually we are accountable to ourselves for what we think and feel and do. The enforced substitution of "I" for "you" is only a technique intended to shake us out of our customary dependence on other agents. To say, *"I can't walk the streets without being afraid I'll be* mugged" brings us face to face with our own fear. The fear is mine; it goes with me as I walk down the street. What does it mean? Where did it come from? What is my own experience of city streets, of going into unfamiliar neighborhoods? What is it that frightens me? How do I feel when I am afraid?

Owning your own statement can be an introduction to the reality of direct experience. Taken together, the various experiences to which we attach as "I" become the profile of our uniqueness, our own living reality. If we are always, as the playwright Edward Albee put it, "painfully awake," we are better able to understand and thus to govern what happens to us. The disowning of the "I," no matter how trivial the circumstances, is ultimately a denial of self, a refusal to take risks on its behalf. Whoever does not accept responsibility for his own self but gives over that responsibility to others, must live as a permanent constituent to an outside authority, cut off by his abdication from the possibilities of change, growth, and true autonomy.

Nor are such vague surrogates the only ones to whom responsibility is abdicated. "I've seen the doctor and he says I'm fine": innocent as this often-heard statement may sound, it is a symptom of the degree to which a doctor may be elevated toward what some wit has dubbed "His M. Deity." Probably nowhere else has our deference toward agents been carried to such an extreme. The modern physician has been made not so much the minister to our physical health as its ultimate and sole custodian. He is our personal ambassador from the world of technological miracles. In his presence we are disadvantaged parties, backward nations, members of a primitive tribe. He is the mighty colonial power, favored by the gods to show up our deficiencies and bring us the word. Or such, at least, is the way many of us treat him—even when he does not ask to be treated that way. The doctor gets his training in a long and expensive educational process; but he gets his authority from us. Seen from this misguided point of view, the doctor comes to symbolize *all* authority—whatever is more powerful than we are, whatever knowledge we do not possess, whoever speaks with certainty when we are in doubt. We make of him that supreme agent, the expert.

It was once said that an expert is anyone who gives a speech more than a hundred miles from home —a definition that now sounds a bit obsolete, with such distances no longer formidable or awesome. But we have not lost our awe toward expertise. Nowadays, with the very air we breathe so continually charged with information, with data we can never digest, machines have had to be devised for storing the facts we cannot assimilate. As the body of current scientific information becomes ever more vast, each day we devise yet another sub-category for the newest specialist to arrive among us. Most of us, however, do not participate in this atomization of data. We are at best observers peering through the laboratory window, waiting for the next revelation to be announced by the white-coated workers on the other side of the glass. We join in the homage to the discoverer without ever completely understanding what has been discovered. But after all, it's the job of those white-coated magicians working for us to understand.

When the inquiry in question concerns us directly, you might suppose that our attitude would be somewhat different. But to a large degree we fail to make the distinction. Adrift on the rising tide of expert information, we have given over not only to doctors, but to lawyers, engineers, politicians, and journalists as well—a whole retinue of agents—the same authority we have accorded the scientist as the acknowledged inquirer into the unknown.

Of all these the doctor is the most telling example because he becomes the expert on a question we do (or should) know a great deal about—namely ourselves. If we see the doctor as magically endowed with whatever is needed to make us feel better, we cede all responsibility to him for our physical well-being. But the burden we place on the physicians' shoulders is one he cannot truly assume. We may ask him to identify a particular cause for what is troubling us; but even when he is able to do so, he is at most no more than a partner in our recovery. It is rarely that the doctor can do more than attend to some dysfunction. What he cannot do is to elicit or educe our power to heal and maintain ourselves. It is to this issue that what is known as "humanistic medicine" addresses itself. The principle of humanistic medical training is to enlist the patient's own strengths—physical, emotional, psychological, and spiritual—in achieving and maintaining health. (It is interesting to note that, at least in one context, the

Greek word *therapeia,* from which "therapy," defined as the treatment of disease, is derived, originally meant "education.")

Teachers likewise can become agents to whom our responsibility is abdicated. Our educational system encourages this, making the student a passive target against which the well-informed instructor aims a barrage of data. The result is that many of us confuse information with knowing. But the teachers from whom we learn most may often not be formal pedagogues. They are the ones who, although they know vastly more than we do, are able to inspire us with the excitement of finding out things for ourselves.

The notion of "agency" serves to emphasize the ways in which we delegate others to do the living for us. Treating life as a show of which we are no more than spectators, we become the prey of a terrible feeling of emptiness, the feeling expressed by T. S. Eliot in describing "the hollow men." Our distress is often vague, and manifests itself in periods of inexplicable fatigue, nervousness, or depleted energy. The sense of meaninglessness, or discontent, develops when we fail to maintain the clear sense of self which can be the only true source of our purpose or destiny. So long as we rely on others—doctors, teachers, or experts generally—to be the arbiters of what is meaningful, we can develop no sense of meaningfulness for ourselves. The function of the agent is to *replace* the one who hires him; he performs for his client, acts for his employers. The agent–client relationship may work in a business setting, but when it comes to the personal self the price we pay for making others our agents is the bankruptcy of that self. When we leave it to the doctor to tell us how we are, or the television commentator to tell us what is important, we are allowing the self at the center of our personal nature to lie dormant, to remain a promise rather than an actuality. The curse of human consciousness is that we *know* when we have abdicated the self and allowed others to live in our stead.

This tendency to abdicate may well be more widespread today than ever before. We are daily inundated by facts, by information that comes to us incessantly, from newspapers, radio, television, films, books, and even the graphic arts. Arnold Bennett in *How to Live on Twenty-four Hours a Day*, a book that is both lively and relevant even though it appeared in the early years of this century, wrote that "newspapers are written in a hurry to be read in a hurry." In his day, newspapers were the primary medium of communication, but his pithy remark can be extended just as well to the more varied and ubiquitous media of our times. It is not the media but we ourselves who endow the "news" with the standing of established truth, primarily because we have lost perspective concerning its function. The news, after all, is no more than a continuing daily record of events. But events have meaning only as we ourselves assign it to them. When we ourselves have been in an automobile accident, or have attended a meeting on rent control, or have seen a play, we need no intermediary to report what we ourselves have experienced. Even in such circumstances, what *happened* is never as important as what *mattered* to us. As the psychologist Robert Ornstein has written, "The eye itself is not a camera, but a selective information gatherer." For us humans, simple perception always has a selective element based on our own values—which should suggest that what is "news" cannot be objectively agreed upon. Real events are only those that resonate in our own personal nature. This is borne out by the work of Albert H. Hastorf and Hadley Cantril in a psychological case study of the 1951 Princeton–Dartmouth football game. Pointing out that in such a setting each side constructs its own reality, they wrote:

> We do not simply "react" to a happening or to some impingement from the environment in a determined way (except in behavior that has become reflexive or habitual). We behave according to what we bring to the occasion, and what each of us brings to the occasion is more or less unique. And except for those significances which we bring to the occasions, the happenings around us would be meaningless occurrences, would be "inconsequential."

This conclusion differs only in being more scientific from a saying of the thirteenth-century Sufi poet Jallaludin Rumi: "What a piece of bread looks like depends on whether you are hungry or not."

Applied to the way we perceive the news as broadcast by the media of mass communication, these ideas bring us face to face with how we ourselves determine what is important to us. In the interest of conserving our personal energy, Arnold

Bennett advocated a precise husbanding of the time given to the newspapers. To the concept of time we must now add that of *attention*—which implies a commitment of the personal nature. *Attention is value-loaded time*—and it is precious.

The trap set by the media is that they do not merely present data concerning events, but presume as well to give value (or "significances," to use Hastorf and Cantril's word) to those events. To a great extent we cooperate in this presumption. What we "bring to the occasion" of the news is often what we bring to the classroom or the doctor's office: the absorptive passivity of a spectator, ready and willing to be catechized by authority. We commission the media to tell us not only what has happened, but also and more important, the significance for us of that happening.

In the media, events are presented as a series of crystallized cubes, displayed before our eyes with the presumed intent of showing "all sides of the question." News stories have a fixed, solidified air of certainty—as though this were a reality to be depended upon. As the technology of newsgathering and reporting becomes more and more sophisticated, the sheer number of events that can be reported to us has grown by geometric progression. So we have come to depend on such reporting as a gauge of reality, and thus our sense of the uncertainty and mystery of the universe is more and more lulled and submerged. What the media give us is an episodic awareness, the illusion of occasionally touching down in the "real world." The medium is not so much the message as it is a *massage.* It reaches out and kneads us a little at regular intervals, as a scheduled confirmation that real life is being lived somewhere out there.

But suppose you were to write your own newspaper, covering not simply what happened, but what really mattered? What would your lead stories have been for yesterday? What images called for a photograph? On which issues did you wish to issue a statement of policy, an editorial reflecting your own deeply held convictions? What in your interaction with other people (your own human-interest stories) was especially funny or sad or otherwise worth recording?

To put together—in writing or simply in your imagination—a newspaper of your own demonstrates the value of codifying experiences with which we are acquainted at first hand. It can demonstrate also that we should not accuse the media of conspiring to make us dependent on them for our own version of reality, reverentially tuning in on their broadcast expertise. This is not to say that we are in danger of losing our autonomy unless we verify at first hand everything that is reported. We would have neither the means nor the time for that. But we can retain the right to assign our own hierarchy of meaning to what is reported. We can read or hear what "they" say without at the same time abdicating the knowledge of what *we* believe.

Bombardment by the media, in other words, need not overwhelm us. If we believe the eye to be a camera, we can live as a camera; if we rely on our own scheme of values, we become able to receive information selectively. The question is not whether we must become victims, but whether we will choose to think for ourselves. It is only when we assign to the media the role of governors and sole dispensers of truth that we become their slaves, rather than their forewarned customers.

To assess whether we make agents of the media, we need to review our reading, listening, and watching habits. Are you reading the newspaper in your role as a stockbroker or editor or merchant—in some aspect of your public nature as it moves and acts in the world? To find out the prices of summer houses, or where to buy a pedigreed cat—as a function of your private nature? Or are you identifying with the official reports of the crime rate, or of dropping gold prices, with a shudder of fear—thus letting statistics displace the "I" at the center? Above all, do you give time and attention to distinguishing among these responses? In modern life, there can hardly be a clearer demonstration of our success or failure than in the way we face the welter of information from the media—our choice between a reality constructed by others and a lived actuality according to consciously felt values and purposes.

Such is our habit of allowing others to become proprietary agents of our living energy that we invoke even the weather. "Rain Believed to Keep Voters from Primary"; "Snowfall Sharply Limits Pre-Christmas Sales." Or, "I can't do a thing when it's so muggy"; or, "It's not the heat that gets you, it's the humidity." How convenient to have ungovernable scapegoats! Not for us Nietzsche's "If a man has his *why,* he can put up with almost any kind of *how."* Not for us, that is, unless we stay awake to the values and needs that make up our true motivation. Every one of us has transcended the weather for a cause— sometimes one as urgent as saving a life, sometimes one as minor as having run out of sugar. Yet between these extremes, most of us live subject to the Temperature–Humidity Index in summer and the Wind–Chill Factor in winter.

Humility before the elements is an appropriate attitude, certainly. In our cosmos, weather serves as a reminder of the vast unknown. There is a distinction worth noting, however, between humility and resignation. The use of the phrase "weather permitting" may be a clue to our subservience. We may be confusing our limitations with powerlessness. It is a mark of health to accept the finite boundaries of human life; but it is a distortion to invent boundaries where they do not necessarily exist. It's true that we can't play tennis or be comfortable at an outdoor wedding in a thundershower; but who has not relished loping through a field in a spring rain, or yielded happily to the enjoyment of being soaked to the skin by a sudden downpour? The weather is simply a condition of the atmosphere in which we live. It may not be controllable; but we can always choose how we react to it.

The same applies to the social weather that surrounds us, the conventions of dress and manners. Taken as a whole, these are all transitory; it is their ubiquity that becomes insistent and that can, if we let it, be intimidating. "It's just not done," we say; or "You can't go there without a tie" (decisions expressed, once again, in the second or third person, a sign that we are abdicating responsibility). Even the greatest iconoclast among us lives in part by customary behavior; radical revolutionaries eat at more or less the same time of day as the authorities they would unseat. Language itself, even adversary language, is a convention. Membership in the human tribe involves for all of us some degree of allegiance to the common way of doing things.

Some conventions, indeed, are almost instinctual. They stem from a common biology and serve our fundamental needs for safety, nourishment, and belonging. These customs spring from those instinctlike urges to which Abraham Maslow has given the name of "deficiency-needs." As individuals and societies develop, conventions become increasingly sophisticated. We agree on laws, on rules of conduct, on definitions of the common good. At this level, too, custom tends to become second nature. Custom and convention serve us, however, only to the extent that we consciously *subscribe* to them rather than unthinkingly *accept* them. Subscription, adherence, commitment—these are the investments we make of ourselves in the conventions we care about.

Emerson wrote in tracing the history of life and letters in nineteenth-century New England, "There are always two parties, the party of the Past and the party of the Future; the Establishment and the Movement. At times the resistance is reanimated, the schism runs under the world, and appears in

Literature, Philosophy, Church, State and social customs." What Emerson could not foresee, perhaps, was a period when the party of resistance could, on the one hand, take on all the rigidity of convention, and on the other, lend itself to commercial exploitation, as we have seen happen to the language and dress of the "counterculture."

Convention and custom surround us on all sides. The sign of personal health is not the degree to which we resist, but the extent to which we are conscious of choosing what squares with our own nature. Custom may permit long hair for males, or wearing a pantsuit to a church wedding; but the mere exercise of sanctioned rights is not half so vital to living well as choosing in concert with our unique personal tastes.

Customs are our servants, not our governors. The concept of tact, for example, need not dictate our relations with others. We choose—at best, we *can* choose—to be tactful or not. We can say less than we mean, respond with less heat than we feel, choose not to argue or engage in conflict, or to invite a confidence. Tact, euphemisms, and downright lying are acts in themselves, for whose consequences we are no less responsible. We cannot legitimately deplore a lack of profundity in someone if by our own behavior we have offered no more than a relation based on small talk. Small talk is all very well; but it is small. When we choose to stick with it, we are choosing the inconsequential. Again, *what* we choose is not as significant as *that* we choose, and that in choosing we listen to our personal nature.

In and of themselves, convention and custom are neither good nor bad. As in all our behavior, only we ourselves can invest a custom with meaning. When what we do is an expression of our beliefs, we are affirming a custom that is *ours*. When our customs conform with those of others, we can be said to have agreed to perpetuate them. The key is choice. What we adhere to with commitment is freely chosen convention; what we follow by habit becomes hypocrisy with a sigh of resignation. The agents we have invented to take over responsibility for us are *our* inventions; and what we have invented we can also abandon, once we realize that continuing dependence on external institutions keeps us from the business of living our own lives.

5.
Conflict and
Crisis

Conscious choosing, then, is one of the marks of a healthy person. This does not mean that the good chooser is infallible; what makes a good chooser, rather, is the readiness to go on making new choices, to welcome the responsibility even in the face of risk and uncertainty. When risk is in the foreground, we may call the pressure to choose a *conflict.* The implication here is that prolonged struggle may be involved, that a resolution may be difficult, and that there is the possibility of deadlock. Conflict-choices, in short, are experienced as a battlefield between opposing forces.

The high drama of feelings in conflict is familiar to us all from the time of adolescence. Living through the explosions of their biological development, with a metabolism that sends them careening from euphoria to despondency, young people tend to experience emotional conflict as a matter of life and death, entailing anxieties their elders see as out of all proportion to the circumstances ("If he doesn't call tonight I'll die!"). These extreme polarizations are not typical of mature adults, however. The resiliency gained through experience means access to more possibilities, enabling us to go beyond either–or to the possibility of both–and.

The most familiar approach to both–and in resolving a conflict is compromise. It abates the struggle, and often does so quickly. We can, for example, decide to live in a less attractive neighborhood for the sake of a particularly desirable apartment, or settle the argument over whether to go to the seashore or the mountains by alternating between the two in successive summers. Such minor, in-the-world conflicts are almost absurdly simple to resolve when approached in this way.

Why, then, does compromise have such a poor track record in human history? Why does the compromise solution so often collapse, to be followed by a second wave of conflict more traumatic than the first? I believe the reason is that compromise works only when no deeply held conviction, no value lodged in the personal self, is involved—when a clear victory by one opposing team or the other does not really *matter* all that much. (Religious wars are so cruelly tragic for this reason.) *Compromise is the strategy for resolving public and private conflict; but conflict that is truly personal does not lend itself to compromise.*

Personal conflict arises when we know at our very core that we must make a choice of such importance that we must in effect *become* that choice—not only in the eyes of those who are affected by it, but also in the way we see ourselves. In personal conflict, the greatest risk is that of being untrue to what at heart we truly are.

Our own identity is our personal truth, "rightness," and authenticity. Conflicts at the depth of the personal nature cannot be resolved by compromise because we cannot give ourselves some of this truth and take away a little of that. Rather, we must find some way to *harmonize* and *balance* the conflicting elements—to arrive at what the psychiatrist Roberto Assagioli calls "the fusion of the poles (of opposites) into a higher synthesis." Assagioli identifies a number of such opposites and their resolution: excitement and depression, synthesized as serenity; blind optimism and fearful pessimism, fused as a clear vision of reality; sympathy and antipathy, resolved as benevolent understanding.

All this may sound hopelessly abstract. An illustration will show how it works in actual experience:

Just eight months after the death of her mother, Mrs. H.'s father, with whom she had always had a close and loving connection, married his second wife. Mrs. H. was shocked at what she considered the unseemly haste of her father's remarriage, though she found the new wife pleasant and attractive. She described her conflict this way: "I just can't be comfortable about it. My folks were married for over thirty-nine years; they had one of the best marriages I've ever seen! I can't get over the feeling that she's—well—an interloper. It's just not right. I love my father, and I like his wife well enough, but I feel *torn*. I know—my mother's dead, and she's not being hurt by this, but . . ." Pulled at one moment by love for her father and a wish to see him active and happy, and at the next by resentment that her mother should have been so precipitately replaced, she exclaimed, "I can't stand these see-saw feelings."

Between the poles of sympathetic attachment to her father and hostile anger over his remarriage, the only possible compromise appeared to be a calculated indifference—to bow out of her father's life, to adopt toward him an uncaring, distant attitude. Mrs. H. acknowledged that she had struggled with this possible solution, but found that she could not bear to think of cutting herself off in such a way. Once she was able to see that her conflicting feelings were not reprehensible, it began to be possible to arrive at a third position—in Assagioli's terms, to "include and absorb the two elements into a higher unity, endowed with qualities differing from those of either of them." In this case, the third position was benevolent understanding.

To arrive at such a "third position," the personal self is obliged to exert its powers by determining honestly the intensity of the feelings that are in conflict, and by choosing to raise the center of consciousness—the personal "I"—to a higher and more inclusive position. But one can only will one's arrival at that point by acknowledging all the demands and priorities of the personal nature. The energy of the self is called on not to suppress the elements of the conflict, but rather to *unite* them in a new reality, the reality arrived at through personal choice.

The following exercise can become a good physical metaphor for the "third position." Stand up, in a position that permits you a full step in any direction. Take a few deep, rolling breaths—exhaling deeply with each one—so that your stance is one of relaxed balance. Now, readying yourself to move one step forward, adopt a position of tense alertness, as if you were a lookout charged with protecting the circle that surrounds you. Next, step forward, holding that stance. Your muscles will have tightened, your brows will have knit into a frown, and your eyes will have narrowed. You may have raised your arms and clenched your fists, or be holding your hands open in the manner of a karate fighter. Your leg muscles will be tight, ready for a spring. Hold this stance for a few moments. Then move back to your beginning position at the center of the circle.

Proceed next to move one natural pace backward, putting your body in precisely the opposite stance from the red-alert posture you have just relinquished. You're about to lapse into complete inattention to what is going on around you. Take that step backward—and let go. Perhaps you will flop to the floor like a stuffed doll. Or you may go totally slack, letting your arms flap and hang loose, as though you were a marionette. Now stay in this position, whatever it is, for a few moments.

As you step forward once again, returning to your normal posture at the center of the circle, reflect on how you might *combine* aspects of the two previous positions. How can you hold your body in such a way as to be at once relaxed and ready to move? Perhaps you will bend your knees slightly; or you'll flex your arms, sensing the vitality in your muscles; or perhaps you will scan the room with your eyes like a searchlight. In whatever way you direct your body to exemplify three attitudes—alertness, unconcern, or relaxed attentiveness—you are making choices. You are demonstrating in a physical way the principle of synthesizing one condition with its opposite. The center of the circle is, of course, a metaphor for your personal self. In the exercise, you have been demonstrating the power of your personal "I" to resolve internal conflict.

There are times when we arrive at a stage that is beyond mere conflict—a point at which we recognize that things are *not as they were, and cannot stay as they are.* This is the point of *crisis,* when conflict is intensified to such a degree that it constitutes an existential threat. We are aware that the choice we make or the course we follow will lead to a transformation of our view of the world—a transformation amounting perhaps to a death of the old view, and the birth of a new one. Such crises, not surprisingly, are accompanied by feelings of fear or acute anxiety. The leap of our awareness exposes what is most negative and dire; we tend to imagine all too vividly the onset of catastrophe. Almost always our view of crisis fits the standard medical definition: that change in a disease which indicates whether the result is to be recovery or death. Instinctively our attention is captured by the graver side of the equation. Since we do not know what to do in the face of death, our response is anxiety. In the words of Paul Tillich, "the threat of nonbeing paralyzes the senses."

How, then, can we reduce crisis to the manageable proportions of a conflict? How do we bring it within the power of personal choice?

First of all, it is important to recognize a distinction between what we designate as *conflict* and what as *crisis*. If the crossroads are familiar, if there are alternatives we have encountered before, we recognize (re-cognize = know again) the turning point as a conflict. Most of us are able to recall being subject to conflicting feelings over the choice between work and play, between completing a task and postponing it, between telling someone we're angry and tactfully camouflaging the fact. Such conflicts occur as by-products of daily living. Whether they occur at the outer layer of our existence, or are indeed "schisms in the soul," we are able to look on them as conflicts if we have faced the same problem at some previous point in our history.

But when events bring us face to face with totally strange, new choices—especially when they involve our personal notions of right and wrong, appropriate and inappropriate, false and authentic—we find ourselves confronted by decisions freighted with an importance that takes them beyond conflict. Great literature is filled with accounts of crisis: Hamlet, Oedipus, and Lear are all depicted as human beings shaken to the center of their being by forces within and outside of themselves, such as confront them with a demand for new and unprecedented resolutions. On your own immediate horizon, examples no doubt abound of men and women facing choices they never had to make before—decisions such as bringing a marriage to an end, thus disrupting the lives of children as well as parents; or some unexpected dilemma calling for a total change in life style or career, of starting over almost entirely.

Crisis as distinguished from simple conflict can be identified by six characteristics: (1) strangeness and suddenness; (2) the magnitude of the choice required; (3) long-range implications, as compared with the generally short-term effect of resolving a conflict; (4) the permanence of the choice to be made; (5) the weight attached to that choice, and its intimate connection with our personal values; and (6) the almost total investment of ourselves required by the critical choice.

Each of us needs a reliable guide for distinguishing a genuine crisis. My own experience suggests a tendency to leap too quickly into calling a conflict a crisis. To illustrate, we can apply the list of six characteristics to an actual situation:

A woman I know was fifty years old, and the only surviving child in the family, at the time of her father's death. She had supposed her seventy-five-year-old mother to have been well provided for by her father's estate. After his will had been probated, however, she was shocked to learn that, aside from Social Security benefits and one small insurance policy, his resources had been exhausted during the course of his last illness. Since the daughter's own children were grown, and her husband's income was adequate, she had been planning to leave her job as a teacher and train to become a paraprofessional health worker. But when she and her husband reviewed her mother's financial situation, it became clear that a substantial amount of money would be needed to maintain her comfortably: the "estate" would no more than pay the rent. Her daughter was thus obligated for the mother's food, clothing, medical bills, and so on. Usually a calm and level-headed person, she became desperately caught up in what she saw as a "crisis."

But was it truly a crisis? That there was conflict between her plans for herself and her newly discovered obligations, there could be no doubt. And indeed she was confronted by sudden and unfamiliar choices involving such major concerns as ambition and the sense of duty. But the implications of what she had to choose were not permanent or long-range; nor was she called on to commit her total being to the solution. She still had the option (which she finally took) of staying at her job but arranging to work four instead of five days a week, so as to begin her training in the health field on the fifth day. She and her husband were able to postpone the improvements on their house for which they had set aside part of their savings. In short, the situation involved a somewhat thorny and frustrating conflict—but not a crisis.

For most of us, since the "way things are" is reflected only by our private and public activities, there is a temptation to think "Crisis!" at every drop of the stock market, without referring the situation back to the personal center, the repository of the values we really hold dear. When crises do occur, rather than dwell on the prospect of a negative outcome, we need to recall that implicit in the medical definition of crisis is the prospect of recovery. In Chinese, the ideogram for the word "crisis" (*wei chi,* pronounced *way gee*) is composed of two elements: *wei,* implying a lofty and perilous situation, distress, misfortune, or danger; and *chi,* denoting an engine, a moving power, as well as motive and opportunity: adding up to a graphic summary of the dual nature of crisis. Since Taoist thought is concerned with the polarities of the universe (the yin–yang principle of non-antagonistic opposites, such as night and day, sun and moon, full and empty), and the flow between them, it is natural to find in a Chinese ideogram this equal attention to both aspects of crisis— as danger *and* opportunity.

Accordingly, alongside the six threatening signals of crisis we should place a parallel roster of positive opportunities for growth and change. Chief among these in any crisis is the chance it offers to reinforce the governing power of the personal self. In extreme situations, as at no other time, we learn that the "I" at our center is finally the only resource we have when the resolve to move forward is required. By passing through a crisis we become more independent, more truly autonomous, less prone to rely on others for support. Along with the increase in autonomy, we arrive at a clearer view of our own true priorities, a revivified sense of what is most important to us. The experience of crisis increases our own store of knowledge both about ourselves and about the world, thus lessening the turmoil of future crises.

It is only through experiencing crisis that we truly grow. Out of the passage through crisis comes the flowering of the self. Crisis can be avoided only by those who refuse to undertake the journey of becoming; for to become means to be always *potentially* in crisis.

A crisis, then, is not simply a milestone marking the obstacles overcome in the environment. It is also the mark of our having come to grips with those creative urges that so often come into conflict or are entirely repressed. The greatest danger we face at critical points in our evolutionary living is that we may not win through to the authentic personal core, that we may fail to will our values into life. On the other hand, the acceptance and integration of crisis into the experience of our unending development constitutes the ultimate opportunity. We must greet crisis as a chance to become something more, in actuality, of what intrinsically we already are.

6.
I Have My Job, But I Am Not My Job

"What do you do?"

"I'm a lawyer. . . . Do you work?"

"Yes, I'm a decorator."

"That must be interesting. . . . What does your husband do?"

So goes the familiar ice-breaking ritual between a man and a woman at a dinner party. Quite apart from the banality of the exchange—whose opening gambit in many countries would be considered rude, if not downright uncivilized—it suggests how often we fail to distinguish between our *work* and our *jobs*.

To work is to perform tasks, to make things, and to interact with other people—all as part of a dynamic process that has a goal. A job, on the other hand, is the abbreviated designation that summarizes a work role. What interests us is not that a person *is* a lawyer or a decorator, but what he or she *does* in that capacity. As a lawyer, does he or she defend persons accused of crimes, or manage trust funds, or write legislation? As a decorator, does he or she specialize in buying antiques for wealthy clients, or in dressing mannikins for Bloomingdale's windows, or in planning small apartments for people with modest incomes? It is not only natural curiosity that makes these distinctions worth pursuing; failure to do so can indeed become the source of much distress and conflict. We tend to identify with the insignia of our jobs—the minutiae of rank, titles, "security"—things we *have.* Yet if we become dissatisfied, we describe our unhappiness as "no longer enjoying what we *do.*" Certainly dissatisfaction with both work and job does occur. The key to dealing with the problem is to make the distinction clear. Is it what I *do* that I find frustrating, or is the job I hold the source of my unrest?

One useful way to clarify this issue, and perhaps to discover a clue to work we might be doing instead, is to keep a detailed diary of a work hour. Select one working hour, preferably one in the middle of your working day. Each day for a week, keep a journal of everything you do during that hour. Include all nonwork activities as well—small talk with your colleagues, coffee breaks, personal telephone calls, writing nonbusiness letters, or simple daydreaming (and what you daydreamed about!)—as well as the details of work you actually did. Most important, record how you felt about what you did. Since you are keeping a confidential record, you are free to be honest about what you found enjoyable, what bored or exhilarated you, what gave you particular pride, what you found frustrating.

By writing up such entries every day for a full week, you will be able to observe a pattern in what you do, and how you feel about it. If you find it hard to remember details, or if you find that your entries tend to be crabbed or inhibited even after a week, continue the diary for a second week, or for as long as it takes you to record with ease and candor the true details of your working hour. The ultimate purpose of this exercise is to discover what you do best and enjoy most. It is one thing to say, "I like working with figures," but quite another to know that you actually relish using the calculator to tote up deductions for a tax return, or in working out the future budget of a new enterprise; that the interview with a businessman seeking advice on bank loans becomes the high point of your day, or that you really prefer the research involved in looking up past rulings on tax claims.

The most likely result of keeping this diary of a work hour will be a series of *relative* judgments about your various functions. You ma, discover, for example, that you are only moderately interested in the spending habits of shoppers, but are fascinated with devising ways to chart the information; or that the most rewarding aspect of your job is the rapport you have with your fellow workers, rather than the particular tasks you are assigned.

The range and priority of your satisfactions at work are the best guide to dealing with its problems. In the terms we have been using, the assessment of its rewards is *personal;* your relations with other workers are *private;* and your job title is an aspect of your *public* nature. Clearly, the decisions you make at the public and private levels of your working life will be soundest when they are based on insights derived from your personal nature. Your diary of a work hour can be an important help in seeking new ways to make your work an authentic expression of that nature.

Certain kinds of work, then, will turn out to offer personal rewards. You will discover, through the self-scrutiny of a diary, the relative value of what may be called the *currencies* involved—such things as power, influence, status, service, learning, and leisure, which turn out to be just as important as the spendable dollars we receive in compensation. We take or stay with a job because of the possibility of earning such prizes. If you are one whose long-range goal is to spread ideas in which you believe, you will find the greatest reward in a job where influence over the minds of others is one of the currencies involved. If your greatest satisfaction is in associating with other people belonging to a certain group, you will be happiest at a job that guarantees association with that group. If your deepest wish is to help others, you will not be happy unless your work gives you such an opportunity.

These relatively intangible currencies, which could be called "intra-psychic rewards," go into the contract we make with the outside world. Like so much in our relations with others, they are often not clear to us until we realize that we are being deprived of something that matters greatly to ourselves. Once again, only the personal nature can be relied on to discover the relative weight of those currencies, to identify the "salaries for the spirit." Carl Jung wrote, "Only the man who is able *consciously* to affirm the power of the vocation confronting him from within becomes a personality; he who succumbs to it falls a prey to the blind flux of happening and is destroyed." He used "vocation" here in its literal sense, as *calling;* but the discovery of meaning and purpose is part of the same human phenomenon: the urge toward self-actualization—or, in the words of Søren Kierkegaard, "to be that self thou truly art."

Respecting the personal nature is important in making good choices in the public and private realms. Many cases described as "career crises" grow out of the inner distress that comes from a sense of having missed one's true calling. The crisis of pain and conflict experienced in connection with a job or with a marriage may in fact be a demand for change in the overall direction of one's life, rather than a merely negative resentment of things as they are. Acknowledging that we can never achieve perfect integration of our own qualities, and still less any control over the random events in the world around us, we can nevertheless keep alive the awareness of which part of ourselves is acting in the name of the whole.

The condition of alienation from ourselves, so

often attributed to the rise of the bureaucratic state, is fundamentally due to the loss of self-knowledge and of responsibility to the self. Bureaucratic tyranny is possible only if its victims cooperate, if the power of the inner self is abdicated rather than actively expressed. It is this heeding of the inner self that accounts for the career of a Schweitzer or a Gandhi. Obviously such men had exceptional gifts to begin with. What we tend to ignore all too often, however, is that their gifts were put to use out of conviction about what was most valuable to them. Centered in that clear sense of worth, they had evaluated their own currencies.

In order to evaluate for ourselves the currencies of power, money, influence, status, altruism, and learning, it is to be expected that we will seek a balance among several or even all of these. Moreover, such an accounting is not a one-time enterprise, but must be repeated at subsequent stages of one's life and career. Although you may not be able to draw a neat pie-graph of the rewards, assigning exact percentages to money, power, and so on, you will see more clearly, for example, that you are willing to work for less money in a certain kind of job because it gives you a chance to move around and meet a lot of different people; or that though a job in research is confining, the challenge of working on tough, complex problems is truly satisfying. You may not be able to tote up these currencies as precisely as the balance in your savings account, but you will know when you are—or are not—receiving adequate pay in "the coin of your personal realm."

Balancing out the ingredients is seldom easy. The habits and priorities of those around you can distort the apparent value of the rewards that are offered. Subtle variations on the old theme of keeping up with the Joneses may deflect you from following your personal self's truest inclinations. Discovering that a friend from college is making $100,000 a year as president of a corporation, or that a cousin has just been elected to Congress, or that someone your age has just won the Nobel Prize for chemistry —such things can throw anyone into a fit of envy or near panic, so that there is an urge to tilt lances with every headline-maker in the news. But in balancing our own system of reward we get nowhere by such comparison or competition with others, whose own inner experience of worth and reward we cannot possibly know.

To bring to consciousness the personal meaning that lies deep within us requires a courageous act of will, and an equally courageous act of acceptance. Willing to become conscious of what has meaning for us, and then accepting the challenge—both are part of hearing and trusting the awareness in us that we can learn only by self-examination. What work is easy and fun, as though you were meant to be doing it? What work makes you feel you are the right person doing the right thing at the right time? What work makes you feel that you are in "overdrive," getting your second wind, oblivious of the time spent on it? Is there a kind of work that gives you the feeling that you are merged with other people in a seamless web of cooperation? Is there the prospect of some accomplishment in your work such as you would want to stand for you when you're gone? Does what you *must* do in your work assignment coincide almost exactly with what you *want* to do?

In reviewing such questions, we begin to see how some aspects of work are also aspects of *living,* whereas others belong entirely to the category of *livelihood.* Making the distinction may help you to make the appropriate choices. For most of us, who do a single kind of work, it may appear that we are engaged only in working for a livelihood. You may look back at earlier decisions (to study law or English literature, or to become a systems analyst), and recognize that even though those early choices were made out of an authentic desire for self-expression, the choice seems to have been the wrong one: you no longer feel right about being what you set out to be. If so, the chances are that the early choice was *not,* indeed, prompted by the need to live expressively, but rather as a promising start in the direction of livelihood, as a guarantee of economic security and status. Although it might seem that the path to true *personality,* in Jung's definition, ought to consist of clearly defined stages, in the complex world around us, the painless unfolding of vocation into self-realization almost never occurs. What Jung affirmed in his statement concerning vocation is that the role of will and consciousness is vital because our "calling" comes most often when we are already beset by what he called the "blind flux of happenings."

At such times, the circumstances that surround

us—mortgage payments, insurance premiums, our rank and seniority, the years we've put in with the company—can appear as overwhelming obstacles to change. Accustomed in ordinary circumstances to juggling money, time, and energy just to keep our heads above water, we may be driven, when the sense of vocation assails us, to describe the job we have as a "trap" or a "prison." Self-realization and self-expression—responding to the sense of vocation —seem quite impossible.

Modern society adds to this difficulty in that it does not encourage us to listen for such vocations. There are experts who can tell us where the jobs are, but not what is the work we were born to do—the work that is both an expression of the personal nature and a path to developing our unique potential abilities. To resolve such a dilemma, we can devise forms of self-examination that make it possible to understand just what choices lie ahead. To decide, for example, whether you should in fact leave the security of the position you have been complaining about in favor of something new, you can begin by making a list of all the positive and negative qualities of the two. Beginning with what is concrete and measurable, you will compare the two on the basis of money, convenience of location, job title and rank, chance of moving up, and fringe benefits. You may add such abstract considerations as the relative degree of challenge, the opportunities for learning. From such considerations you can then move to yet another level, asking such questions as these:

Which job will offer more in the way of mystery and unsolved problems?

In which will I meet more creative people?

Does one job offer more chances than the other for helping younger people develop their abilities?

In which job would I and my colleagues laugh more?

Which job would give me a better chance to bring order out of chaos?

In which would I have more things to learn in the next year?

Is there something quite unique in either job—something that makes it quite unlike any other?

Will one job give me a better chance to make pleasing or beautiful things than the other?

Will one job give me a chance to see justice done, or to see virtue rewarded?

Will society or the environment be improved more by my taking one job rather than the other?

In which of these jobs will I feel more alive?

Is there something in either job to feel really lucky about?

These questions are, of course, not practical. They measure nothing really tangible. But they have the virtue of suggesting still other questions, of inviting exploration rather than flat and final answers. They cause us to examine our work choices in the light of goals outside our own obvious and immediate interests. They help us to plumb that part of ourselves that identifies with deeper needs, goals such as truth and beauty and justice—needs that are associated with meaningfulness in our lives.

We need to be honest about acknowledging that in established occupations, careers, or professions, time is seldom—if ever—given to such values. I heard one unhappily perceptive young man say of his work that he felt as though he were at the Twenty-third Street subway station and could see all the way to Seventy-seventh Street—and that he hated the notion of a life-trip spent entirely in a subway tunnel. Such distress is not the decree of fate, but a signal. For those of us who have already committed years to one profession, feelings of terror are likely to accompany that signal; a feeling that starting over is now impossible, or that "giving up what one has" would cost too much. Such are the pains of growth and transition. But if you can resolve the internal conflict by recognizing that certain needs of your personal nature are not being met in your present work, you will have identified the source of your frustration and unhappiness. You should be able to use that same insight and honesty to assemble and define possible alternatives. You will be asking questions to which there are no final answers, of course; but in so doing you will be going forward as you go inward to meet your destiny, your calling, your vocation.

You will discover, in short, that if it is to bring you personal prosperity, your work must serve not just your body and your mind, but your spirit and your dreams as well.

7.
Going South When You Have Been Going North: Some Case Histories

What changes when a dentist becomes a sculptor? Or a successful book editor becomes a marine biologist? Or a sophisticated city couple moves to a farm in Vermont?

The first thing we notice, of course, are the cosmetic differences—the open-throated shirts and jeans instead of the three-piece suits, the smells of home-baked bread in the kitchen, the Land Rover in the garage instead of the Granada. We know these to be symbolic, the exchange of one set of uniforms and insignia for another. Surely, we say, denim does not liberate the human spirit any better than flannel, or three-risings brown bread enrich human creativity more deeply than a loaf from the supermarket. We have had too much experience of mere surface appearance to be persuaded that these outward changes bespeak any "real" change. Our friends, we are sure, are not different at the core, but have merely become different consumers.

What we want to know is how our friends are making out in their new professions or their new houses. Are they happier? Do they feel more "fulfilled"? Is life richer for them in some way? Are they personally thriving? On these questions there are usually two common judgments: either we think that they are fools—or we envy them. On the one hand, we are inclined to suspect that a turnabout of this order is a form of escapism, or a sign of some endemic restlessness. (Perhaps, if we are hyper-analytical, we even relate that restlessness to a subconscious fear of death.) Or we see in these people a midlife revolt against sameness and convention, an echo or a repetition of explosive adolescent rebellion against all authority. We are sure our friends will "take their misery with them wherever they go." On the other hand, we may have an equally positive interpretation of their adventurous plans: we are convinced they have indeed "found themselves," that they are courageous nonconformists, that they are not afraid to go after what they want—that they have truly changed.

Let us turn now to some men and women who have made that sort of decision. Let us determine from their stories whether any of such total and extreme judgments are correct.

THE BIG MOVE

For seven years Mrs. T. had worked as traffic manager in the art department of a large advertising agency. Increasingly, feelings of anger and depression had centered around her job. "Now it's so boring I can hardly describe it," she told me.

At the time I met her, Mrs. T. was forty-seven. Her two daughters were in their twenties, her son was seventeen, and she was consciously preparing for the day when all three would have left home for good. For years, she told me, she had "dreamed" of starting a small yarn and knitting shop of her own, thus becoming fully involved with what for many years had been simply her avocation. "My problem," she explained, "is that I've never been action-oriented. I've always been able to see what I should do, but it seems to take dynamite to get me to do it."

To an outsider this sounded contradictory. Mrs. T. was an energetic woman; she did her job well, ran a busy household, and had an active social life. It was only when she contemplated the "big move," as she called it, that she saw herself as a dreamer rather than a doer. She spoke in great detail of the difficulties involved in starting a shop, of the competition there was, of the unfavorable economy. Asked to sum up in a sentence why she had not ventured to act on the project she dreamed of, she answered, "I guess it's because I've never been a self-starting person."

Up to a point, of course, this was the statement of a responsible person. Mrs. T. was acknowledging that in any such venture she would have to supply the energy, make the commitment, take the risk. But instead of taking on the responsibility, she had allowed herself to foist it onto an agent—her own record of hesitation. She had filed herself away under the heading of "always dreaming, never doing." Not until she began accounting to herself in detail all the many things she had actually done, and done well, could she see how she had been building up a mosaic of "little reasons" for the defeat of her own plans before she started. Having confronted the habit of saying, "I never could . . .," or "I always . . . ," she was able to break through the imaginary impasse and put an end to her frustration by leaving the job that had come to bore her.

CONFLICTING CURRENCIES

Several years ago I met a young nurse who was experiencing a conflict over her personal values. At the age of thirty-five, she had already spent half her life in giving service to others. While she was still in high school she had taken her first job, a menial one in a hospital for the chronically diseased. She then went on to nursing school, and on her graduation accepted an assignment with a medical missionary group in Burma, where she encountered not only abject poverty and endemic disease, but also political unrest and outbreaks of guerrilla warfare. Her one reprieve came when she was sent for advanced training to a larger city, where she worked in a modern hospital. At the end of her term abroad, she was transferred to the United States, where she continued to work at assignments far less lucrative than most jobs in the nursing profession, though living conditions were of course much more comfortable than what she had known in Asia.

At the time I met her, she was in great uncertainty over what to do with her life. It was now clear that having been rewarded only in the "personal" currency of service, she both yearned to be well paid for what she did, and felt guilty about that wish— regarding it as a betrayal of her lifelong commitment to the unfortunate. When she did permit herself to "think about the unthinkable," she was able to see that her wish to be better paid did not mean turning her back forever on being a helper. She decided to give herself six months to explore the world of moneymaking, and became a saleswoman. In that six months she earned more money than she had in two years as a missionary nurse. But during that time she also came to realize that what had been important to her as a field nurse had been not the self-deprivation, but the work itself—the care and healing of sick and injured people. At the end of the six months she clearly understood what her priority was, and took a job with a community health center in Boston. She would be earning less in dollars than her sales commissions had brought, but the rewards to her personal self would be greater.

The issue for her had turned out to be simple

and clear-cut, perhaps more so than it would have been for most of us. But the lesson is clear.

BRANCHING OUT

An architect described himself at the age of forty-four as feeling "dried up, bored and restless." His choice of a career had been clear to him in his late teens, and he had never been conscious of more than fleeting dissatisfaction as he made his way up the ladder of his profession. Even now, he could speak with animation about the pleasure of designing a house, and the special satisfaction in seeing his drawings translated into a real building. He lived well, and had made enough money to provide comfortably for his wife and three children. His restlessness did not appear to rise from the job he was doing.

But then, almost as though he were revealing a guilty secret, he mentioned that he was also designing and building furniture, which he simply "put away" or used as "extra pieces around the office." These pieces were admired by his colleagues and by others who saw them. The most ingenious design was a modular desk with almost infinite possible combinations. His cabinet work was marked by patient attention to fine detail: indeed, the architect said, the true reward for him was in "making small things perfect." He spoke of a fantasy he kept having: he would chuck his lucrative practice, move to Vermont, and spend his working time in producing "just a few pieces a year," to be sold by mail order or to tourists.

Here was a man who had already heard and responded to a personal urge to go beyond the demands of his job. The critical first step, however, had led him into an impasse: he saw his options only in completely polarized terms. He must either settle for remaining an architect or throw it over entirely for the life of a bucolic artisan. For him the coin of the realm had become the status and money he derived from being a successful architect, reinforced by the influence of his ideas on others. He was not ready to give up totally the pleasure he still took in the *functions* of being an architect. He had looked on his work in making furniture as a "closet" activity, a hobby, since it did not fit the work-and-reward system to which his professional career had accustomed him. But as he analyzed his experience in designing and making those perfect pieces, he began to see that this work had meaning for him far beyond mere recreation. He could then begin to plan how he might carry on both activities—one for the rewards it offered, the other to answer the emergent demands he felt as an artist. He came to realize that as he treated his one-time "hobby" seriously, it would be considered seriously by others—that he could actually sell a few pieces a year out of his New York office, while he continued to design buildings—but took fewer commissions as an architect.

The realization that it is possible to diversify in such a way can come as a shock. Having grown up in a world that honors single-track specialization, most of us early in our lives were being urged to concentrate, to develop one particular skill. We were warned especially against having "grasshopper minds," and variety was depicted as a distraction. Even in ordinary commerce, "professionalism" is emphasized, less as a standard of competence than as a badge of specialization: the aim is to become a C.P.A., not just an accountant; a Certified Life Underwriter, not just an insurance man. Trying to work at more than one thing is apt to be regarded as dabbling or dilettantism, the mark of a shallow or frivolous nature, in a society where the specialist is regarded as vaguely more serious than anyone else.

The only approved exception to this rule is the one occasioned by financial emergency. A second job made necessary by extraordinary medical expenses, or the plight of an unemployed relative, is seen as legitimate. It is then assumed that the time you are giving to the second job would otherwise have been spent in leisure. If you take on a second or third kind of work "just because you like it," that is acceptable for so long as you treat it as a hobby or a form of recreation. The notion of working seriously at more than one thing, so as to give expression to more than one part of yourself, brings you up against the strictures that go with the vaunting of specialization. Such is the force of this cultural norm that if others do not sneer, or criticize us for spreading ourselves thin, we are likely to feel the conflict within ourselves. Thus the architect felt compelled to rationalize his furniture designs into a hobby—so that he and those around him would not see it as a threat to his success as a specialist. He took this risk when he decided to branch out; but in doing so, he added richness to the texture of his living.

The urge to try something else is likely to be concealed at first, then acknowledged with distrust, then fantasized about in secret. Eventually we may begin talking about it with family and friends—and often this stage is as far as it goes. The logical next step would be to test the possibility in the real world —a project that might be called "psychic moonlighting." The dominant currency here is likely to be self-education. Such "moonlighting" ought to be just as honorable as driving a cab to pay for your husband's tuition in a graduate course, or waiting on tables so as to be able to take singing lessons yourself. In such tentative branching out you are paying the same respect to the need to *become* as to the need to *survive.*

THE EXHILARATION OF RISK

Eliot C. made two startling changes of direction in his life before he was forty. At thirty-one he was already a full professor of economics at a major university; he had written two books—a scholarly one on finance in the Industrial Revolution and a popular history of money—and was now doing research on what he called his "big project," a book advocating a return to the gold standard. Eliot and his wife Laura —also a successful college teacher, with plans to write a history of women in medicine—were happily established in California, with no discernible problems. It could not have been any ordinary frustration that caused Eliot to alter his career. But as he put it, "With all the projects we had going, and even though things were fine on a day-to-day basis, I had a gnawing feeling that something was missing, that I was supposed to be doing something else. Not instead of teaching and writing necessarily, but in *addition* to all that. . . .

> One weekend, Laura and I were on a camping trip. During the night a sudden storm erupted and the heavy rains washed away part of the walls of the ravine where we had pitched our tent. The usual trails for getting out were eroded, too, and about a dozen of us seemed to be trapped, with the threat of being inundated if the ravine collapsed any more. We were all frightened, and not sure what to do, but knowing we had to make a move—and fast. I realized quite suddenly, standing there with torrents of water coming down on me, that I had to take charge, that no one else had any idea how to get out. I had never been in the Army or anything, but I heard myself begin to bark out orders, and get everyone busy with packing up gear while I explored for a possible safe way out of the gully. When I found a way that seemed to give us a fair chance, I herded the rest of them up the hill and through a protected part of the forest.

> When we got home, I was exhausted—but exhilarated. Not just with the ego-pride of being a 'leader,' but because I realized I had felt thrilled and galvanized by risk and danger.

> Then almost immediately I saw the connection with my life in general. . . . There were no *risks* in what I was doing at the college. . . . Now I knew that I needed and wanted more risk than that in order to feel I was using *all* of myself—not just my mind and my storehouse of information.

> Shortly after that, a man who had read my money

book called me. He was a trustee of an experimental college in Oregon. . . . They needed to raise a great deal of money to keep going, and they needed an almost instant overhaul of the administration . . . He offered me a job as the vice president of the college —at exactly what I was making as a teacher. But he promised me a free hand to raise money any way I wanted—not just by petitioning foundations and governments, but with public programs, adult education, concerts, publishing—anything. The stakes were vital: either I could raise enough money in two years—or at least demonstrate that the money-producing plans would generate the needed income—or the college would fold. My God! it felt like the rainstorm on the ravine! . . . The next morning I resigned my teaching job. We were out of the house and on our way in twenty-two days!

For two years I really scrambled. While Laura kept working on her book, I was trying everything I could think of that a college could do to raise money. (We weren't quite so rich ourselves; Laura's teaching salary was gone, and we had to live a lot leaner. No new clothes, we ran our old Volvo up to 92,000 miles, and we went into a period we called "food de-emphasis," with lots of stew and fish—and we saw a lot fewer movies). It was marvelous! I worked ten hours a day, and on most weekends, too. After a while I felt as if I were battling for my own survival, not just the college's. . . . It was hard, and I didn't love every minute of it, naturally. Sometimes I felt like a door-to-door encyclopedia salesman, or even worse . . . But I was pulled through those times by remembering that whatever crass stuff I had to do, I really believed the college was worth saving. . . .

Even before I knew we were going to make it, though, I knew I would have to move on. . . . So when it became clear that I had done the job they asked me to do, and they offered me a nice teaching spot—even with a small raise—I didn't jump at it.

This time there was no dramatic, symbolic storm to help me see what I needed. I knew I had to keep active risk in my life, but this time it would have to be in the cause of building something new, not just preserving a faltering institution someone else had built. How did I know what to do next? You may not believe this, but I made a list—a horizontal and vertical checklist. Across the top I wrote what I wanted from my work: I remember, I wrote "risk" first, then "money" (the amount Laura and I had learned to live on), then "something new," then "using what I know," then "learning new things"; next to that I wrote "San Francisco or L. A.," because both Laura and I felt we wanted to live nearer a big city than we had. Finally, I wrote "five years" . . . We had begun to talk about having children and that reinforced the idea of looking for at least a five-year base. . . . Through the college I heard of a number of jobs, but none of them fit our blueprint. Then one of the community mental health people I had met in my money-raising job came to me with an essay he had written about the need to start what he called "mobile rap groups." It was the outline of a plan to send vans around the neighborhood spots with trained counselors inside them—a place teen-age kids could go to talk about their problems. His idea was sketchy, and he had no notion what it would cost, what the legal implications were, how to handle community relations and that sort of thing. I remember him saying, "Come on, teacher, teach me. Educate me on the costs of doing Good Works." We made a kind of barter deal then, because I asked him to let me come to his training group for counselors—in return for doing the figure work on the project.

Well, you know the rest. The project became a partnership. I learned how to get grant money from the city and the state, we worked out some of the problems in manning the vans, and now we have five of them all around L. A. county. I'm not just the administrator, either. I work with kids seven hours a week in the "rap-vans." Oh yes, Laura got a tutoring job as soon as her book was finished, so we're still breaking even—and we have our chart checked off in every detail—for now, anyway. Of course, there are still three years to go on our five-year plan. . . .

One important lesson of Eliot's odyssey is that he did not turn his back on his own history. He did not become "Jim," but remained "Eliot." Feeling that he must "move on," he did not assume that doing something new and different required him to discard his past achievements altogether. His story demonstrates the value of capitalizing on our previous experience. The temptation to belittle and discredit what we have been doing is to be resisted. Honest work, by definition, is never unworthy; and our past can and should be part of what we bring to whatever is before us. Thus, Eliot knew a great deal about money, both in a theoretical sense and in terms of day-to-day planning; and both kinds of knowledge went into the success of his risk-taking new ventures.

CHANGE COSTS SOMETHING

Donna T., a stock market analyst, at the age of thirty-six was earning over $21,000 a year, in a business dominated by men. Here is her story:

When I was a kid, I already knew one big fact about money—we never had enough of it. Morning, noon, and night our family conversation centered around scrimping, and not wasting. My father used to say, "With us it's either being poor—or poorer." The first time we read about wages and profits in social studies class, I made up my mind to use school as a place to learn about making enough money to shut off those memories of bickering, screaming, and slaving. I was a good student, and I zipped through college and graduate school on scholarships and summer jobs as fast as I could. When I first started working full time, I lived at home, and put as much as I could into the family treasury. Things were better for my folks when we kids grew up, but by then, my mother and father were exhausted. Finally, they both retired, and thanks to their pensions and Social Security, they had enough to get by.

Shortly after I finally moved into my own apartment, I woke up one morning and realized I had never stopped working long enough to take a deep breath and look at what I was doing—and *why!* I think I had never questioned that my goal was anything but not to be screamingly poor. And here I was, not only not poor, but with my own care, all paid for, and with, of all things, $5,000 in a savings account. I was downright rich! Or was I?

From that time on, I asked myself that same question every day. And I began to see that I might be O. K. on money—at last—but I began to hate what I was doing to get it. I became painfully aware of how abused I was in the office, not just because I was a woman (though, God knows, there was plenty of brutality in that), but also because I was the youngest person in the department, and because I was a work-horse, and somehow the piles of stuff for me to do were always bigger than everyone else's. I saw what my work-addiction was doing to the rest of my life —I had only a few friends, had had a tough time really connecting with men, and I was always saying, "I don't have enough time." When I was alone I sometimes looked at my savings account book and cried. Finally one day I just tore it up into little pieces.

Then I knew I had to do something. But *what?* I didn't have a hobby, I wasn't a ballet lover or a theater freak. I hadn't traveled anywhere I might get a new idea, or even see a dramatically different way of living.

So I decided to push myself into something new. An aunt of mine was a teaching nun on the staff of a church-sponsored nursing home. I went back up to the Bronx of my childhood and asked her if I could do volunteer work. I started almost right away, reading to people, helping them walk around the grounds, feeding the really feeble ones.

I met a doctor and nurse team up there whose job was to come in and do periodic checkups of the old people. One day the nurse asked me if I had ever done any yoga. Even though I told her I had only gone to classes for a few weeks, she invited me to help her teach some of the older people who were in pretty good shape some exercises she had adapted from her yoga experience. Wow! was that fun! We were fumbling around a little, and I was afraid and embarrassed. But after a few sessions we were really helping those people breathe better and teaching them how to relax, too. By the time we began experimenting with weekend body movement workshops, I was so turned on I began to have fantasies about being a nurse and doing it all by myself.

Then I had a dream in which one of the surlier boss-

men in the office was showering me with piles of
IBM punch cards, and screaming at me at the top of
his lungs. Suddenly, in the middle of the yelling (in
the dream) I reached up through the pile of card-
board, grabbed this guy's wrist, and began to spin
him around like I was a Kung Fu champion or something. He just kept turning and turning over my head
in slow motion, and I was cackling with laughter like
an old Chinese sage!

Well, after that I knew it was time to get out. I had
a pretty clear idea that I wanted to train some way
in something like yoga or body movement or relaxa-
tion technique. Through my friend, the nurse, I
looked into all sorts of places—some straight college
stuff in geriatrics, private institutes, and the like. As
I got more and more excited about the prospects of
learning to become a professional helper, I also got
more and more panicky. Every one of those courses
cost a lot of money, a good deal more than the for-
merly great treasure-trove in my battered savings
account passbook. They cost a lot of time, too, more
than I could spend if I was to have the only kind of
job I knew—hard, slugging work from nine to five
every day. My reaction to all this was to go into a
massive depression; I reacted just like a "Depression
Baby," haunted not just by my own memories of
being poor, but also by every story I had ever heard
or read about desperate, fallen men selling apples on
street corners to feed their children. I damned near
gave up any idea of getting out of Wall Street.

One Saturday, my nurse friend and the doctor no-
ticed how low I was and offered to hear me out on
my dream of changing careers—and the terrors that
were keeping me from it. When I had gushed it all
out, the doctor said to me, "You know, if I had a
problem like that, I'd bring it to you." "What are you

talking about?" I said. "Are you crazy or what?"
"No, I mean it," he answered. "It's a money problem,
in fact it's a moneymaking and investment problem
you've got—and you know more about investments
than anyone I know."

We really got into it at that point. Every time I raised
an issue like the rent on my apartment, or the cost of
gas, he'd answer by saying these were all "business
expenses"—except that I was to be the business, not
some aerospace corporation. He kept pushing me to
think of it as investing capital in myself—selling the
things I could do without, "lending" myself the balance in my savings account, borrowing from the
bank or from friends to finance part of what he kept
calling "the new venture."

When I began to analyze it that way on my own,
with all I knew about industrial companies who do
that sort of thing with millions and millions of dollars, it all made sense. After all, if I chose to go to a
formal university for academic training, I'd apply for
a "tuition" loan, wouldn't I? And if I chose to go
somewhere for training that wasn't covered by the
state tuition-financing law, why couldn't I get that
loan from myself, or my friends, if I had to? "Tuition"—that's the word that broke the problem's back
for me—that and the idea of seeing my change of
professions as an investment enterprise.

I know that to a lot of people, that probably sounds
silly, but once I could see that I was the most important thing I could ever invest in—or gamble on—I
just treated it like a problem at the old office.

Donna decided to apprentice herself to a well-
known teacher of a body-awareness and movement

system in New York. She quit her job in Wall Street and for two years she supported herself as she had planned—on her own savings, with one formal bank loan, and a small personal loan from a friend, plus some income from free-lance typing she could do at night at home. (She even reduced her training costs by doing the bookkeeping for her teacher's institute.) When I last saw her she was a part-time staff member at the institute where she had trained, had a private clientele of her own, and was running groups in several senior centers in New York City. She was not quite up to her previous income of $21,-000, but she was living comfortably, and had paid back all but $1,500 of her loans.

It would be too easy to say that Donna had suddenly decided to be "good to herself," that she had merely stopped struggling to be stable and solvent (and to avoid her parents' poverty) and started to work for the purpose of feeling good. Like many of us, Donna had, early in her life, adopted the tunnel vision that characterizes those who have known true poverty. Her story reminds us that we often continue to do battle with old enemies even after the dragon has been slain. But beyond the distress to which her singlemindedness had led her, there is a deeper lesson in Donna's experience: all of us must labor to *cope*, but if we would grow *beyond* coping we must make changes that will enable us to unfold more richly.

Donna also teaches us that we should neither ignore nor panic over the cost of making changes—the personal "tuitions" she spoke of. The price of change need not be in dollars, but it must be paid in one currency or another. We may have to pay in status, by taking on work that is less "glamorous," or involves us with fewer famous people; or we may have to move away from the consensually defined centers of power in society—from Wall Street to a senior center in Queens. We may have to give up some of the influence we have, as Eliot did when he left off teaching large numbers of students in favor of an administrative job. We pay for change just as we pay for material things. However, we set our own psychic "moving costs"; only we can decide what we will give up, and for what goals. Once we know these tuition costs—what currency they are expressed in, and how much of them is involved in our new contracts with ourselves, the rest, as Donna put it, becomes a "management problem."

As with Eliot, Donna did not change into someone else when she made her big leap. She did not invent a new personality or design a new shell to house the person inside. For her, change was not a matter of invention but of discovery. Her experience also shows how the fear of change is *necessarily* a part of the process. The confirming realization that the change we have made is right can come only after we have made the leap. If your sense of purpose is clear, and if the change you envision grows out of your own personal center—rather than being motivated merely by a desire to escape present frustration— you will find an increase in the energy available, and a new flexibility in adjusting short-term tactics, at once coping with current obstacles and breaking new ground for the next stage in the continuing evolution that is your true self.

A PROCESS, NOT A CONDITION

The gift of life is the gift of energy. We live through action, movement, *change.*

At any given moment we may say, "Life is great," or "Life is rotten," according to the conditions that surround us. These highs and lows are no less real for being the result of outside forces. But to see them as the whole of life is to mistake the shadow for the substance. The healthy, thriving, self-actualizing person has the quality of movement, not a fixed state of being. As Dr. Robert Hoke has written, "The phenomenon of health is a living activity, not a product. It is not something to *have,* but a way to *be.* It is a procession, not a possession."

Change and growth at the very core of consciousness are not only to be accepted, but indeed actively sought, by the person in search of self-realization or self-fulfillment. Recognizing our evolutionary character, acknowledging our own "unfinished" quality, is a precondition for successful travel in that direction. But we must not fall into the error of identifying self-fulfillment as a finite, reachable goal. As human beings we are at all times involved in the dynamic process of becoming; we are, in Theodore Roszak's phrase, "unfinished animals," participants in our own, and the world's, evolution.

We can move *toward* maturity, *toward* self-actualization, *toward* personal prosperity. Along the way we may reach a plateau from time to time—a new or higher level of functioning—but that plateau is merely a way station at which we pause for a view of the possibilities that lie ahead. As Jean-Paul Sartre put it, "Man is, at least in part, his own project." The process of change, the dynamic sense of autonomy as we "make ourselves in our own image"—this is true freedom, and it is all the richer for being part of a drama larger than ourselves.

The thriving person is able to accept change wherever it may occur—change in his own body, change in the perceptions of his innermost nature, change of careers, change of location—even the change that comes accompanied by a sense of loss. In all of nature and experience, change is inescapably present. We are organically enmeshed in the process of change—the unending cycle of day and night, of tides and seasons, of birth and death. And to all of these, the thriving person responds without illusory wishes that it could be otherwise. We cannot engineer our response to change. Joy or grief, the need for courage, do come as we respond to our circumstances; and when they do, we rise to the occasion as we *trust* the promptings of the personal self, seeing in what happens a reminder that we are the *creatures* as well as the *creators* of change.

We know ourselves to the extent that we know the direction in which we are moving. And in a sense, for the thriving person, that direction is always the same: all roads lead us nearer the center of our own being.

To sum up:

Change is the way we build our own future.

Change is not, however, the transformation of

oneself into something entirely different, but rather its expansion into a more vivid realization of what we already are.

Change, both within ourselves and in the world we inhabit, is inevitable and unending. We can choose to see the possibilities it offers as a reflection of our values—or simply give ourselves over to it passively, like travelers aboard a train we cannot stop or control.

The desire for change is almost always made up of the *push* of distress, and the forward *pull* of a new goal. If you are drawn *primarily* by a magnet of possibilities, the chances are 80–20 in your favor. If you are *primarily* driven by distress, the odds are also 80–20—but against you.

The urge toward change is invariably accompanied by the fear of changing. To stand still requires the courage to defend what you now are; to risk change requires the still greater courage of discovering what you might become.

The price of change is as real—and as unique—as the necessity for change. Yet that tuition is finally the only investment worth making—so long as you know what it is, and are willing to pay it as the price of growth.

Change is growth when you use your energy and fortitude in the service of a value you hold dear. A clear personal purpose is the adrenalin of the spirit, arming us with new strength to live up to our destiny.

My north may be your south, his east her west —if each of us is on a path of change that goes toward the heart of the personal vocation within us.

8.
Love Is Action

For the first few months of any human life, the world and the self are one. We do not distinguish ourselves from parents or siblings, or indeed from the rooms that surround us. In other words, we have consciousness but not *self*-consciousness. We just *are* hungry, or wet, or drowsy, or happy. It is only later, at some time between the ages of three and four, that the words "me" and "mine" take on significance for us. When they do, the new world of personal pronouns can be unstable. Margaret Mead reported the following exchange between a bright four-year-old and his teacher:

> STUART: *Me* is a name, you know. My name.
> TEACHER: *Me* is my name, too.

94 · Choosing and Changing

> STUART: No, it's mine. How can it be yours? I am *me!*
> TEACHER: I am, too.
> STUART: No, you are not *me.* You are you. (After a pause) I am *me* to me, but you are *me* to you!

We can see in this confrontation the beginning of a lifelong pattern of knowing oneself to be separate, but related to people "out there."

Every connection we make in the world is, potentially, an experience in loving. Friendship, partnership, business and social intercourse, chance meetings with strangers: all of these expose us to the possibility of exchanging some portion of that energy we call love.

Love, whatever form it takes, is more than a feeling. It is an act. Loving another person means to support and endorse what that person is now, and might become. Love is thus an act of will: we choose whether to risk it; we choose the way it is to be expressed. When you dare to listen to the inner voice of your personal nature, you reveal the core of your own personality. When you risk being loved by another person, you turn this act of self-revelation outward, letting your newly discovered self be seen by the loved one in all its incompleteness in its struggle to evolve.

Making this act of self-disclosure to others only potentially leads to love. When Martin Buber says, "All real living is meeting," he is suggesting that our intercourse with the world is the encountering of our public surfaces with each other. Most "meeting" ends with that superficial encounter. Only the act of will permits that encounter to progress from public meeting, to private acquaintanceship, to personal love. As Rainer Maria Rilke said, in one of his letters to a young poet, "Love consists in this: that two solitudes protect and border and salute each other."

Every meeting can turn into a loving relationship; but the form that love takes is never the same, even when honest self-disclosure and the will to risk love are present. Thus we have come to speak of "forms of love": romantic love, courtly love, Platonic love, erotic love, friendly love, the love of God, and so on. Love is an action; it is the *expression* of our feeling toward an object, a symbol, a person, a body, or an idea. All forms of love reflect the unifying aspect of love, the attempt to merge with something outside ourselves, in order to complete ourselves. From Shelley ("Love, thou art my better self") to Lorenz Hart ("You have what I lack myself"), the urge to find in another person the imagined but un-realized possibilities of goodness, talent, beauty or worth has been the recurring theme of our love songs. Love finds its expression not in independence, nor in dependence, but in interdependence. That in-terdependence makes a loving relationship one in which the whole is greater than the sum of its parts. We love, therefore, not only as an expression of feel-ing for the one we value, but as an affirmation of living, as a way of enlarging life itself.

Since our ability and our will to love are so great, we each find that we need many kinds and forms of loving connections in the world. In any such form, we have the authentic experience of love only if we can make the *act* of loving the genuine reflection of the *feeling* that springs from the core of our being, that resides in the heart of our personal nature. The *feeling* of love may terrify or exhilarate or engulf us; but our *response* to the torrent of love is a matter of choice. We may fall to our knees in the face of love, or embrace the one we treasure, or turn away in dread; only we can know, if we are fully *self-conscious*, whether the choice we make is appropriate for us. Our spontaneity, our joy, our gesture of tenderness and respect, even our fear—all these are part of our unique psychic makeup. We owe to the feeling of love the same obligation of singular response that we owe to every special value we call "ours." Whether it is our child, our mate, our colleague, or a cedar tree that stirs in us that feeling of warmth or devotion or urge to foster, we have a choice: to risk acting on the feeling of love; or to withhold action, to risk nothing.

Monumental as the stakes are, we make such choices in small gestures and intimate behaviors, in subtle rituals and habits. Under the light of full consciousness, we can control and direct these gestures toward the goal of acting authentically on the love we feel.

The dynamics of love are mysterious; but there are some things we can say about the *acts* of love— the acts that confirm our feelings with words, gestures and behaviors that we can control. Let us look at some ways these acts of love occur: the love of a man and woman; the love of a parent for a child; the love between partners in an enterprise; and finally, the undifferentiated love we might feel for our universe and the unknown, anonymous people in it.

MAN AND WOMAN

The love between a man and a woman is both *needy* (since the other fills some lack in ourselves) and *needless* (since we love the other just as he or she is, without regard to what he or she might do for us). We love, too, the promise we sense of the other's unfolding. Often we are aware that we can see that promise in our beloved, while other people seem not to see it. Love is not "blind," as the saying has it, but quite the opposite. Love gives us enhanced vision, a sensitive perception of the core of the other, as if we were able to see into a seed, and imagine it blossoming as a flower. Love is experienced as a flash of understanding; for the briefest moment, we see a vision of a completed painting, where only a rough sketch appears to the neutral eye. With this gift of loving vision comes the urge to devote ourselves to what we see, to nurture the blossom within the seed, to protect the canvas in order that the envisioned painting might emerge.

While we are under the spell of this enhanced vision, our love leads us to the edge of a great risk —that love may turn into arrogance. Once we foresee the beauty, talent, and worth that might emerge in our loved one, we may become dictatorial custodians of that new image. We may try to master and control our beloved, in the name of this ideal image; and our expression of love becomes not endorsement, but judgment. We may attempt to dominate the unfolding process, to push it here, to hold it back there. We become not personal lovers, but private sculptors, insisting that the clay of our beloved's personality conform to our vision of what he or she *ought* to be.

When that happens, we begin to speak in the language of judgment: "You never . . ."; "You ought . . ."; "You always . . ."; "Do you realize what you're doing?" We have confused the early privilege of love —the gift of seeing that the other holds *a* great promise—with our own egotistical notion that we know *what* that promise is, that we possess a secret blueprint for the other's growth. We make our loved one into a project, not a person.

The special foresight of love enables us to know not *what* is going to happen, but *that* something will happen. Love makes us a witness to life itself; it lets us share in the revelation of a self outside our own. If we exceed the role of the privileged observer, we become manipulative and intrusive; we use, rather than love, the treasured person.

To reveal your deepest personal nature is an act of trust. By entrusting the loved one with your own cherished values, you make him or her the keeper of your better self. When the disclosure is mutual, there is another kind of risk: each may come to idealize the other, to make the other into a myth, to treat the other, ultimately, as unreal. If each acts as the curator of the other, the "better selves" tend to become rigid, to petrify, to become like statues.

Such idealization of a loved one is trust and respect run wild. When it occurs, the idealized person becomes intimidating. So a process begins of tailoring one's disclosures, of editing whatever one says—of behaving *for,* rather than with, the other.

When such formalities take over, the loved one moves out from the heart of our consciousness to an area inhabited by private friends with whom we have only limited encounters. Under the strain of keeping one another on pedestals, even private communication becomes empty. Love recedes into mere admiration.

In those marriages where there is misery because *nothing happens,* the emptiness represents a withdrawal such as takes place when idealization replaces love: statues do not touch. To an audience they may appear to be the perfect couple. The problem of such marriages, someone once said, is that they become a "struggle to work out the problems of being perfect for each other."

Something like this occurs when two people base their love on what they call "shared values." What holds them together, such a couple may be heard to say, is that they are "both working for the same goals." An admirable statement in itself, it may also be a sign that the intimate disclosures, the unfettered play, the mutual joy in nonsense, the animal merriment—all that is "minor" but ineffably human between lovers—has been foresworn in favor of public achievement. Of course, the genuine dedication of such couples to a common project may indeed produce enduring results. But it may also be that the project becomes not a *result* but only a *symbol* of their original commitment. Shared values may constitute both an attraction and a bond at the beginning, but they will not replace a love that is attentive also to the being and becoming of the other.

Just as high aspirations can dilute or inhibit the

expression of personal love, so can entrenched notions of love itself. Its awesome possibilities can lure us into false heroics: love must be choired by heavenly voices, not whistled in the kitchen; it must be told in proverbs, not in laughter. The impulse to give our love expression in play is too often, as we grow older, relegated to the attic of our minds along with memories of tree houses and electric trains. Mature love does carry grave obligations; they are implicit in our taking responsibility for another human being. But we must not allow maturity to become a false god, a ruler that shuts down our senses to the delight in absurdity, or in savoring the small pleasures of smell and touch and form.

PARENT AND CHILD

It was the counsel of Lao Tzu that one ought to

Be parent, not possessor
Be attendant, not master.

Whether any of us can entirely shuck off the pride of identification that comes from knowing that our children are "flesh of our flesh, bone of our bone," is doubtful. Can one *will* to be an undevouring mother, a father who governs without ruling? Throughout human history, the answer appears to be No. But many have gone some part of the way toward the goal of finding how to love and guide their children without overwhelming them.

To admire and even adore a baby is easy. What is not so easy is to *respect* it. The infant is so small, so dependent, so weak and vulnerable. When the baby is our own, we have total power over him. As he begins to stand and move and explore his world, our child is clearly learning and taking risks at every moment. We find these discoveries amusing—but still not worthy of respect. Too often we love the child because he is ours, rather than for the unique nature that is unfolding before our eyes. Unable to say, "I have that child, but I am not that child," we express our love as possessiveness—forgetting that the role we have been given is not that of a ruler but of a gardener, entrusted with the task of fostering growth and health.

Fostering our children's growth requires us as parents consciously to detach our own identities from those of the children themselves—to see them as persons, not possessions. Even when the child is very young, we can do no more than point out the danger of fire, pulling small hands away from the flame until one day the lesson has been learned. That this lesson may nevertheless be forgotten years later, when the twelve-year-old neglects to use a pot-holder in taking the brownies out of the oven—this is, to put it bluntly, no affair of ours, except in the role of administering first aid. Love makes us feel the blister on our child's hand as though it were our own; but now the only appropriate response to that feeling is sympathy. Love makes us a witness of the transition from dependent learner to independent mistake-maker—a witness but not any longer a participant. Difficult as it is to love children and leave them alone, we owe them that trust.

One thing that makes trust possible is greater knowledge, such as can come from doing something rare among parents: from *listening*. We think we know our children better than anyone else. How can there be anything about them that we do not know? The answer is that though we have sired or nurtured the physical child, part of the child's nature goes beyond genetics. To have a child means eventually to meet a new person—who, regardless of whatever profound resemblance to ourselves, is not only separate but different. If we listen, we can learn the nature of those differences. And in learning about what makes that child "tick," we may also see our own world from a different perspective. A child is able to see many things directly, as they are in essence. There is much for us to learn here if we permit ourselves to listen with open-minded respect.

While they are young and dependent, children remain citizens of that peculiar society called the family. As adults, as governors, we make and enforce the laws, keep the economy going, and provide a tribunal for resolving conflict. We occupy a powerful position—for a while—and we must examine the way we use it. If we are, for example, frustrated by not having had power in the outside world, we may easily turn our household into a military camp or an occupied territory. A far cry from the careful gardener, tending what grows there!

Parents also abuse their power through manipulation, using children as pawns in domestic power games. We may see a "hard" parent deny a plea for ice cream; whereupon the "soft" parent approves the treat, thereby showing up the spouse. Or we may see how one parent, following a still unresolved quarrel with the other, will show remorse not directly but by directing tenderness and warmth toward one of the children. In such a case, feeling deflected becomes retaliation. For love expresses itself in action, and that means it must be communicated to its object. The temptation is always there, but we can consciously choose not to make use of our children as the agents of our own tangled purposes.

BROTHERS WITHOUT A HISTORY

One of the richest opportunities for translating love into action is through a project undertaken and shared with someone else. Such a partnership becomes an opportunity to learn from and also to teach another person, as we might have done with a brother or sister—and without the obstacle of unresolved childhood conflicts and jealousies. A good partnership can become an enlargement of what is good about belonging to a family.

Not that it is often easy to arrive at the coordination needed to work well and lovingly with another person. There is a tendency to overemphasize complementarity, to say, "We work perfectly together because Bob is great at details and I hate them"; or, "Mike is Mr. Inside and I'm Mr. Outside. We're the perfect combination." Such division of labor may indeed be efficient, but if we fail to look beyond it, the partnership will ultimately founder. Each of the partners will come to believe that the work he does is more than fifty percent of the whole —and to resent the situation accordingly. Knowledge and trust, such as go with love, will have to be mustered to avoid an ugly outbreak of conflict. If the division of the work load can be based on preference, no matter how odd the resulting mixture of functions, the satisfactions of being a partner are enhanced. Such a division can be arrived at only by honest encounter of the same sort that enables a man and a woman to live together in harmony.

If one partner says, "You'd better see the customers; I've never sold anything in my life," the response ought to be a direct one: "Is that because you don't want to?" It may turn out that the diffident partner would in fact like to deal with the firm's customers, but hangs back out of reluctance or timidity. Approached in such a way, partnership can be a joint fostering of each other's development.

Another opportunity opened by partnership based on love is to learn about the power of initiative. The partner who originates something, however small, takes on a special role and responsibility. In a partnership that is kept open by trust and self-disclosure, we discover how the igniting energy of initiative can alternate between the partners. In this way, initiative is prevented from becoming a political advantage—with one partner blaming the other, at some later date: "It was your idea to ship six of them in one carton! You got us into this, now you get us out!" Blame and fault-finding are largely eliminated if the partnership embraces the other's mistakes as well as his positive triumphs. Permission given to the partner to attempt something new is also a guarantee of permission to initiate actions of your own without fear of recrimination. Since the success of any project depends on information and skill, the more intimately we know our partner, and permit him to know ourselves, the greater the chance of shared success.

Partnership is also ideal for learning the lesson of detachment: how to let go. If we are to live with change, we must learn to give up, to lose, to let go of things even as we learn the arts of getting and keeping. A loving partnership will include a respect for the other's right to leave, to move on to some other place, even to another partnership. Since true partnership is characterized by approval and trust of the other as a person, and not just as an entrepreneur, approval and trust will extend to respecting the partner's need to change. Through a genuine partnership we learn that persons are more important than projects; and that what men initiate they must sometimes also abandon. Since this is true of all human connections, the lesson is vital to our balance, and helps us to accommodate to the inevitability of change. If we have come to understand a working partner intimately, we have also prepared ourselves for an understanding of other changes that may be in store for us.

By all this I do not mean to imply that partners in an enterprise must love each other if that enterprise is to succeed. Love—the urge to trust, to care for, to respect the development of another person— cannot be forced or legislated. But a partnership that is based on closeness and a shared goal can be a favored setting for experiencing yet another form of love. To have succeeded in a project without knowing more of one's partner, and oneself, through the medium of love—this is to have missed a rare chance of increasing one's personal prosperity.

LOVING AT LARGE

The fact must be admitted, if love is defined as active and not merely a feeling of good will, that we do not have time to love everyone or everything in the world. Oppressed people in a remote place, orphaned children in a war zone, an endangered region or species—any of these may nevertheless inspire us with a feeling of obligation, an urge to help somehow. How can we act on such feelings?

If we are committed to discovering the self at our own core, and to the values of that self, our first step will be to act as directly as we can on what *matters* to us most. Not only will we go to work on our home turf, as preferable to complaining that we cannot reach out to everyone; also, we will look for the work we know ourselves to be uniquely fitted for. When we volunteer our time, then, we will not merely say, "Can you use me?" This does not mean, of course, that we should refuse to do menial work —help clean up a flooded town, fight a forest fire, or be prompt in coming to the aid of a neighbor in an emergency. It does mean that when we work for a cause, what we do is done best when it reflects our particular talents.

Giving money or old clothes to a welfare organization represents affiliation, not commitment. Our contributions to the Audubon Society or the Sierra Club or the NAACP identify us with issues and programs. But if we limit ourselves to that kind of philanthropy, we are expressing *public* support for causes—not personal love. We live in a time when the issues concerned with energy resources, pollution of the environment, living space and the growth of population, are all so overwhelming that we tend to make a gesture of public affiliation and leave it at that, just hoping for the best. Yet the whole principle of ecology is the ancient wisdom that "everything is connected to everything." We, too, are connected to everything. Our car, our oil burner, our local hunting laws, the stream that runs through our property—all of these are links in a single, unending chain of connection.

With so many causes "out there," it is often easier for us to send a check for a child in Vietnam than to do something about the child who is eating lead paint off the walls in a slum ten blocks away. Each deserves our help; but until we can attend to both, we are well advised to make our acts of love as local and as personal as possible.

When we act on our love for the world, the watchword should be directness. Buber's "all real living is meeting" means that our daily life is filled with encounters that are potentially loving—if we but allow them to be. According to the old joke, "I love humanity; it's people I hate." Yet the humanity we say we love is right there in the waitress, the colleague, the bus driver, the man riding with us in the elevator. And how seldom do we encounter them as representatives of humanity! For the most part, we do not even see them. We see the menu, and talk to it: "I'll have the London broil," we say without a glance at the woman who stands there, finding no reason to look at us either. All day long our gaze is reserved for those persons we *have* to look at. The others amount to a kind of public furniture.

The mutual gaze of two persons is the fundamental human connection. Yet this primary act of disclosure and acceptance is lost to many of us in our dedication to *getting around* other people rather than confronting them as persons. We look at a great many people, but see very few. Yet by not seeing them, we forego a chance to explore our kinship with humanity.

No less an obstacle than this quasi-blindness to knowing and being known is the way we *hear* other people. We have made conversation itself into an adversary act: "I'm going to hold you to what you said"; "Give me your word"; "That's not what you said yesterday"—such locutions demand of others a precision we do not always exact from ourselves.

In Taoist philosophy there is no concept equivalent to what we call lying. For the Taoist sage, there is only an obligation to hear the truth, to "believe the truthful man, and also believe the liar—thus all become truthful."

There is a lesson here for us. By learning to interpret rather than cross-examine, we can avoid much of the hostility and distrust that arise from workaday connections. If we could hear the conditional phrases and the hidden intentions that are mostly left out of what people say, we could avoid much of the disappointment and anger that result from listening defensively. To the repairman's promise to be there tomorrow morning, we could supply the qualifying "if I can make it." When you ask your daughter what she did in school today and she answers "Nothing," you would then hear what she is really saying: "Nothing I want to talk about right now." Overhearing a friend tell someone else that she is thirty-five, when we happen to know she is forty, we will understand that she is really saying, "I'm afraid of losing my looks."

Recognizing these truths in what we hear, we will go on to remember that we, too, have made promises and then not kept them; grunted a monosyllable to a provocative question; or fibbed about certain personal embarrassments.

Listening *for* the truth rather than *to* the version others happen to present means that we are in a position to trust those others, not because they are infallible but because we share their imperfections, because we recognize what a struggle it is to be perfectly consistent and honest. Holmes Welch writes, "When the Southerner says to the Eskimo, 'Yesterday was a chilly evening,' the words 'chilly' and 'evening' mean different things to each. All of us are to some degree Southerners and Eskimos to each other."

Listening for the truth makes human understanding, and therefore love, more likely. When we hear others use words imprecisely, we remember that their true meaning can be determined only in context, and then only as we apply our own patience and insight. Since listening for the truth is so difficult, we become obliged to give others more attention, more respect, more care—all of which are prerequisites for loving.

The clearest example of how to act on our feeling of love for the world is to be found, ultimately, in the behavior of children. "Children have no sense of ugliness or beauty," someone once said. It is that innocence of all judgment, that view unclouded by prejudice, that allows then to approach and enjoy the world so freely. The young child alive with curiosity, who does not back off from the drooling of a puppy, who wonders what is behind the face in the mirror, or what is in Grandpa's watch that keeps it ticking, or where the flower came from—gleeful, eager to learn—is willing to love everything in the world. As adults, we tend to delight more in our children's mastery of a task than in such artless exploration. For us, curiosity has become equated with utility. With strangers and new acquaintances we deal only in the same familiar, predictable counters: "What do you do?" "Where did you go to college?" "We used to own a Fiat too." So long as our wondering about others stays at a level of such constrained superficiality, we will never really get to know them. And without knowing them at a deeper level, we can never love them. We cannot truly respect one who has been inventoried in our minds according to such labels.

For too many of us, the loss of wonder and the fear of showing curiosity are the price of having grown up. We are afraid when a party shows signs of turning into a "heavy evening," or of getting into dinner-table talk that is "too intellectual." And so we never learn whether that soft-spoken lawyer has a conflict over representing child-murderers, or discover that his wife, introduced as "the filmmaker," has a background in theology and is concerned with understanding the roots of evil in human behavior. To show curiosity has come to mean being "nosy" or "pushy"; so we keep on tap a collection of discussible trivia, repressing our own deeper interests in favor of acceptable small talk. We have made information more valuable than knowledge. We no longer want to know things, only to know *about* them. To know rather than simply know about calls for the risk of remaining open to the strange, the unfamiliar, the uncharted—an openness that is the door through which love might enter.

The acts of loving are always acts of will. Love requires us to declare ourselves, commit ourselves, and risk ourselves—all acts that come from the personal nature. Love needs no validation from outside. Its only utility is that it affirms life, expanding not just our physical world and our perceptions, but our inner solitudes. Through love we put not just ourselves, but life itself, to the test. As Rilke wrote, "For one human being to love another: that is perhaps the most difficult of all our tasks, the last test and proof, the work for which all other work is but preparation."

9.
Health
Equals Whole

A middle-aged business executive in New York City who is found to be suffering from an abnormally accelerated heartbeat—clinically known as tachy-cardia—may be told by his physician that his condition is the result of a subconscious response to stress. A middle-aged man in Hyderabad who raises or lowers his heart rate at will, returning to normal whenever he wishes, is a living demonstration of the voluntary control of internal states. The executive is called a patient, the Indian is called a yogi.

Elmer and Alyce Green, pioneer researchers in biofeedback training, point out the meaning of this distinction: some people, like the yogi, have learned *consciously* to "turn on" and "turn off" certain physiological processes. Others, like the executive, have learned *unconsciously* how to "turn on" those processes, but not how to turn them off. The principle behind the two cases is in fact the same: that the mind plays a part in internal physical behavior, just as it does in one's public and social behavior. In each case, we have isolated just two factors for study: the executive's reactions to his environment and his heart rate; the yogi's conscious volition and *his* heart rate. By isolating these functions we infer, inevitably, some connection between them, one that can be confirmed by repeated experiment in a controlled situation. We would be wrong, however, to deduce from our findings that we are dealing in either case with the *whole health* of either man. For these functions, though they may exhilarate us with visions of total autonomic control of bodily processes, are in fact imbedded in still larger processes—what the executive might call his life style and the yogi his philosophy. These patterns are matters of choice, acts involving the personal will of the living man. Each man might easily be taught the *technique* of the other, but it is unlikely that either would wish to trade completely with that other. We would, in other words, have to know a great deal more about each before we could use the evidence of their heartbeats to establish the relative "health" of either.

There is no such thing as physical health—or mental health, or psychological health, or emotional health. None of these aspects of a human being can be divorced or cut away from the wholeness of the person. Health is the actualization of *all* that is present and potential in us: we are, at any given time, healthy to the extent that we are manifesting all our inherent possibilities.

The word *health* in fact comes from the same root as the words *hale* and *whole.* Thus its very etymology suggests the way our development should be measured. Body, mind, feelings, and spirit are all part of one whole. They do not act upon one another as subject and object, like billiard balls striking one another, from first one and then another direction, but are inextricably interwoven, a fabric of interaction. To treat them separately or sequentially, as agents of stimulus and response, is to reduce the human being to a mechanical model composed of interchangeable parts. We may isolate a physical or mental function, we may alter a person's behavior with drugs or through surgery, but we cannot pretend that in so doing we are dealing with the whole person. René Dubos, in *Man Adapting,* puts the matter this way:

> The components of the body-machine *react with* the environment, but living man *responds to* his environment. In fact, man's responses are not necessarily aimed at coping with his environment. They often correspond rather to an expressive behavior and involve using the environment for self-actualization. Health in the case of human beings means more than a state in which the organism has become physically suited to the surrounding physico-chemical conditions through passive mechanism; it demands that the personality be able to express itself creatively.

The creative expression of personality is just another way of describing the process of becoming a whole person. Clearly, a soundly functioning body is *one* aspect of that expression, but it is not the entire expression. A healthy human being may be one with a withered hand, who uses what he has in the way of a sound body to express his authentic purpose, to work for what he believes to be true and important. The expression of the personality, as we have seen, is the function of the private and public natures in accord with the values and goals of the personal nature. Whole health, then, is using what one has in *all* his human systems to express those values.

Physical health is, of course, the most palpable evidence we have of the state of the organism. Our bodies are the outward structure of our public natures, the surfaces exposed to the world. And in the body is the brain we use to formulate the language of thought and feeling. The gift we call life is given originally to those bodies, and we share with everything else in the living kingdom the biology of life-force. Being material, the human body is our primary connection with the world of matter.

The fact that our development originates with a material form does not, however, entitle it to the primacy it tends to assume. The human body does not remain like the roots of a lotus plant in the mud, but presses toward flowering in the manner that is peculiarly human. The body *contains* the promise of life in man, but this promise cannot be fulfilled by the body alone. To remain attached to the body as the sole confirmation of one's existence, to consider its tone and functioning as the unique source of health, is to remain anchored in a kind of sensory infancy. You *have* your body—but you *are not* that body. Your obligation to whole growth calls on you to respect it, to not abuse it, to know its needs and idiosyncrasies, to care for it as the vehicle of your connection with the world.

Going back to the executive with the accelerated heartbeat, let us look at another question. It is likely that at the time when Bruce Jenner won the decathlon at the 1976 Olympic Games, his heart rate was abnormally fast. Obviously it is possible for the human heart to sustain this alteration for brief periods. Can we say, then, that along with the yogi, Bruce Jenner differs from the executive only in that he has chosen consciously to speed up his heartbeat? Or should we not rather say that what we have discovered is how all three men *choose* to deal with their bodies? It seems clear that our bodies are indeed subject to our personal intentions—are available to us for the purposes we define and to which we commit ourselves.

Concerning the executive the question arises, of course, whether his condition might, if it is not treated, lead to a fatal heart attack. But what is it that is to be treated? The quickest way to reverse his symptoms—the evidence his body gave us of not being healthy—is to provide a drug to modify his heart rate. If we go beyond his symptoms to deal with the stress that appears to have caused them, which stress shall we treat? How, indeed, do we know just what in his circumstances causes the stress reaction? And if we are to deal with the whole set of those stimuli, what shall we tell him to do: "Slow down"? "Try some other line of work"? "Divorce your wife"? "Stop worrying about your son"? Or should we perhaps take a physical approach to his symptoms, and prescribe for him a bland, sodium-free diet? Should we go further afield, and refer him to an Oriental physician, whose prescription may include a program of herbs, or even acupuncture?

Each of these tactics could be defended as a way of trying to restore the executive to good health. Yet, given his typically complicated life, it is likely that for the present we can do little more than alleviate his symptoms, with the possible side effect of drawing attention to the surrounding factors *we think* may be involved. In so doing, we have defined health as a limited problem to which there is likewise a limited answer. So long as we confine ourselves to modifying one physical phenomenon in any of a dozen ways, we affect such a man only physically. His health, viewed as the entire process of his growth and development, still eludes us.

This limited approach defines the current state of medicine and health care in general: they are concerned mainly with what Dubos calls "physical adaptation by passive mechanisms," and what they do best is largely confined to the curative and preventive: to repairing some sick bodies and preventing illness in others. No consensual vision has yet been arrived at of how to approach what has been called "promotive medicine"—a philosophy of health care in which fostering the growth of whole persons is a goal equal to the job of restoring the disabled and the prevention of epidemic disease.

Some ways in which curative, preventive, and promotive medicine might work together are suggested by a personal experience I had in the course of writing this book. One Saturday, after several days of high fever, periodic chills, and severe headache, I checked in at the emergency room of a country hospital. A thorough examination, including chest X-rays, revealed a slight case of pneumonia. The physician who examined me recommended bed rest and prescribed an antibiotic drug, Erythromycin. But there was no immediate relief for my "skullcap" pain; the discomfort was so great that I could move my head only with difficulty.

Three days later, I spoke with my colleague at the Center for Health in Medicine, a physician and a close friend, whom I had called earlier and who had urged me to be examined in Connecticut, where I was working. He now urged me to come into the city, so that he might examine me and rule out the possibility of meningitis. He explained that the severity of my headache must be due to extensive inflammation of the three-layered membranes, called *meninges,* that cover the skull. In New York, my doctor friend examined me again as the physician in Connecticut had done, and also put me through a series of exercises involving my legs, arms, and shoulders, designed to stretch the meninges. If these movements had brought on severe additional pain, further tests for meningitis might have been indicated. My friend repeated the tests several times over, and each time the result was the same: I had no more pain than I had while lying entirely at rest. In fact, after about five hours all my symptoms began to recede, and I felt considerably better.

At that point my friend asked me if I would give him his allergy shot. Knowing that he had a sensitivity to ragweed pollen, he was now preparing himself for the onset of the ragweed season. The effect of the shots was to hyperstimulate his body's immune responses by injecting pollen in increasing doses over a ten-week period. His body would then produce antibodies to combat the pollen, so that by the time ragweed was most prevalent in the air, he would not have to suffer the characteristic allergic reaction.

After I had given him his shot, I began to laugh. "Look at us," I said—"both of us trying to make promotive medicine an integral part of American health care—and here we sit. I'm loaded with Erythromycin and we've just loaded you up with ragweed pollen to insure you against sneezing three months from now!" Exploring the irony with more seriousness, we came to see that we were indeed examples of our own contention—that curative and preventive medicine have their value for bringing yourself to a kind of "base-line zero." Most people think of that base-line as health; but my friend and I, with an increasing number of others, believe that health is what happens *above* the base-line. *Whole health* to us is what you do with yourself as a creative act when body, mind, feelings, and spirit are in harmony.

In my own particular case, believing that life

above the base-line is my own responsibility, I added deep-breathing exercises and meditation to my daily schedule. (The breathing exercises are described at the end of this chapter.) As the subject of my meditation I took my friend's description of what was going on in my lungs as a result of infection: the "dead-end" sacs (alveoli) of the bronchi were at least partially filled with debris—white blood cells and pus—so that the air I breathed in could not oxygenate—that is, the oxygen I inhaled could not go through the usual "gas exchange," by which carbon dioxide goes out as one exhales. What his description suggested to me was a curbstone drain clogged with leaves, so that rainwater on the street could not drain away.

During my daily meditations I would visualize the opening up of clogged spaces, clearing away material that blocked an opening. I concentrated on images of getting rid of whatever was obstructing the air spaces in my body, which in normal circumstances are free and receptive. When I could not get a clear picture in my mind of this cleaning and clearing process in my own body, I would return to the mental vision of clearing away a mass of leaves from the opening of a drainage grate.

LIVING ABOVE THE BASE-LINE

What lies above base-line zero is the *future*—the moment, or day, or year in which you are to live the life that is given you; whereas what we usually call our health is the momentary condition of the *present,* of which the measurements are, for the most part, fixed and static readings, most of them negative: that you do *not*, for example, have a body temperature in excess of 98.6°, you do *not* have a viral infection, you do *not* have an inordinate amount of sugar in your blood, and so on. You are adjudged healthy when no known disorder is present at the time you are examined. The absence of such visible disorders is what enables the physician to say to you, "You're fine."

In all fairness, the health-care practitioner is doing the best he can. His commitment is to help you maintain your foothold on that base-line; and if he sees health as this neutral point, it is only because he knows his limitations. He can help sustain life, but only you can turn that life into productive living.

All the help we can get with our physical, mental, and emotional systems is of this order. Those trained to assist us can assess only what they see and hear at certain isolated points as our time intersects with theirs. When a physician or a psychotherapist recommends, say, that you cut down your office schedule to four days a week, he is not telling you what to do with that fifth day, but is only throwing you back on your own resources to decide how to use it.

To view your health as the condition of your body at a particular moment is to ignore the dynamic character of health—that it is a process, not a condition. We must remember that up until the last moment of biological life, we possess a residue of health. It is that residue that empowers us to choose how we shall die. The capacity to choose our behavior in a future moment—even the final one—is the way we express whatever health we possess.

The example is extreme—but it reminds us once again that what lies above the base-line zero is *the unknown*. We are moving into uncharted territory, knowing that there will be risks and periodic crises, turning points in our development. Becoming ill can be one of those crises. Medical people can tell us, when we are ill, what causes the fever or headache or the feeling of weakness. But they cannot tell us what is going on in our lives that needs attention: whether, for example, the congestion in our lungs is part of a larger pattern of congestion in our energy, or part of a repressed fear of completing a task, of changing jobs, of falling behind in paying the bills. At one level there may be the urge to finish an assignment; it may even be possible to talk about the difficulties and opportunities that seem to lie ahead. We may not act on that urge because of fear that there may be dangers we have not anticipated, or because of fear that we might fail. But we may not be ready to acknowledge those fears. It is at this juncture that our bodies take over, and do the fearing for us. In becoming ill we become *legitimately* unable to do what we have promised ourselves.

The trap in all this is that our symptoms are so real and so painful that we crave above all to be relieved of them. I say "trap" because this preoccupation may be a distraction from the other, non-physical aspects of our illness. The recovery of bodily comfort is one goal of "cure"; recovering the will to live out our personal intentions and our plans is another. Illness, then, can be a time for reexamining our goals, values, and priorities, and for assessing the way we put ourselves to their service. Being sick relieves us of the burden of moving toward the unknown future; what we want most when we are sick is to go backwards, back to the way we felt (in our bodies) before disease took over. We now marshal our energies to restore the "good" condition of yesterday, but not to move forward into the unknown challenge of tomorrow.

Health above the base-line is also characterized by *activity:* not mindless running about for its own sake, but purposeful activity growing out of self-defined goals. We all know people whose time is taken up with "things to do," but who reveal in rare moments of repose the unhappy feeling that "life is empty." Filling or killing time with activity is not in itself evidence of the whole health of which we are capable; rather, such a pattern usually signifies the reverse—an evasion of the unique demands of the personal nature. A healthy way of confronting disease is to discover why the body is resisting the move forward, why our physical system shies away from the challenge of self-expression.

We can say, "I'm not working on my book right now because I have pneumonia. As soon as that's cleared up, I'll get back to it." But we should also consider the reverse—the possibility that, in fact, we contracted this illness because we were not doing the work we have assigned ourselves: not only the tasks others expect us to perform, but also the work of expressing our own personal identity, our own values. The vigilance that is usually applied to the condition of the body should be addressed no less to such questions as these: Am I using my own special strengths in a way that expresses what I believe myself to be? Have I found a purpose outside myself—a person, a project, a cause—to which I can devote myself not merely for public rewards, but because of the reality in myself that it expresses? Do I trust my own hunches enough to act on them, even though that action may fail? Am I doing what I do—at work, at home, in the world at large—simply because it is what I did yesterday, or is there newness and freshness still to be explored in those places, and in my relationships there?

Questions like these challenge the activist in us, the maker and the doer as well as the planner. They do not presuppose genius or exceptional strength. They challenge us to use what *we* have and are, not merely for the sake of movement, but of fulfilling our own unique destiny.

Uniqueness, too, is in what lies above the baseline of neutral "health." Who, for example, is healthier—the 300-pound strong man who lifts a thousand-pound weight above his head, or the 116-pound jockey who brings a thousand-pound horse across the finish line in record time? We cannot say, except in a relative way, which of these two is stronger, since clearly neither has the *kind* of strength to accomplish the same feat as the other. The wholeness that is health cannot be measured by "objective" standards, but only by the optimum expression, in each of us, of our special configuration of qualities.

Health defined this way is the goal, in the physical sense, of the "new therapies"—systems such as Integral Yoga, the Alexander method, Feldenkrais body and movement awareness exercises, the Oriental schools of T'ai Chi and Aikido, and many others. Indeed, long-distance running, jogging, and other "conventional" sports activities are now being taught as part of consciousness training. Through such disciplines, under the guidance of qualified teachers, we may learn how to function far above our usual level of performance. For the most part, they are based on the release of the body's inherent energy, on teaching the student not to strain his body, but through conscious control to let it do what it knows best how to do. These systems are "physical" in the sense that the body is the instrument of technique; but in each of them the role of the mind is to *allow* the body to move, not to force it.

The body-oriented humanistic therapies are, in effect, the other side of the coin of psychosomatic medicine. Whereas medicine, informed by the lessons of Freudian psychology, can establish the connection, for example, between certain allergic conditions and mental conflict, the "new therapies" are showing how mental concentration can relax the muscles and make the spinal column more flexible. Whereas medicine is concerned with the cause of dysfunction, the body–mind systems are concerned with what may be called "psychosomatic health."

To go beyond simply explaining the mind's role in bodily ills is to begin to discover a greater potential autonomy than we had thought possible. But even as many lessons of these systems can be integrated into our daily living, we remain body-bound so long as we conceive our development as human beings to be a matter of increased bodily coordination. Along with learning how to slow our heart rate or lower our temperature we need to be aware of *why* these physical feats are of value to us—their part, that is, in the uncovering and confirming of what is uniquely and personally ourselves.

What lies above base-line zero is *living* itself—active, risk-taking movement into an unknown future.

BREATHING EXERCISES

The Rolling Breath: Sitting or lying comfortably on the floor, place your left hand on your lower abdomen and your right hand high on your chest, just below the throat. Take several deep breaths as you would ordinarily, but try to exhale more deeply than usual. As you repeat this a number of times, you will probably notice that even when you exhale deeply, your abdomen is not much involved in your breathing rhythm. You will probably also be aware—through your right hand—that your chest is doing most of the work as you inhale.

Now, try to make your breath still more rhythmic. Start by *distending* your abdomen as you inhale, pushing it against your left hand. Then "roll" your breath up into your chest, pushing it against your right hand. Exhale very deeply—as deeply as you can, and then make a little extra effort to exhale even a bit more. Repeat this, slowly, once again. First breathe into your left hand, then up into your right —and then exhale *very* deeply.

The exercise may seem awkward at first, almost a reversal of your usual breathing technique. So try it again, breathing first into your left hand, down low, then up into your right hand. The deep, deep exhalation is extremely important to the rhythm. According to an old Hindu proverb, "If you learn how to exhale properly, the inhalation will take care of itself." This is so because the inevitable cycle causes us to want to "repay" our lungs with whatever we withdraw through exhalation.

After you have done a number of rolling breaths, you will probably notice that as you exhale, the muscles in your abdomen will tighten and "collapse" inward. Conversely, when you start your deep breath, you will be able to distend your abdomen quite fully. This exercise can be done, after you are familiar with it, sitting up, or in any situation, throughout the day. The subjective effects of this exercise are almost always pleasant. You will feel more relaxed, calmer, more at peace. After five or ten minutes of breathing in this way, you will feel refreshed, ready to take up a new activity with enthusiasm.

Breathing Yourself Warm: For when you want to be working out of doors even though it has become uncomfortably cold, here is a breathing exercise that will help. Sit quietly and get into the rhythm of the rolling breath described above. Now close your eyes, and as you continue breathing deeply, visualize with your mind's eye a tube running down through the

center of your body, from head to pelvis—a per-
forated tube that permits air to be channeled into all
parts of your body—out through your shoulders,
along your arms, and into your hands; through your
hips down your legs and into your feet. Visualize,
with each deep exhalation, the part of the breath that
is moving through the openings to the outer extremi-
ties. Feel it as gentle air, sending warmth to the ends
of your fingers and toes. Continue breathing in
deeply, sending warm exhaled breath to all the parts
of you that were chilled. Continue this regular in–
out breathing, increasing the warmth with each
breath. We are accustomed to blowing on our hands
to warm the skin; what this exercise does is to
breathe a more pervasive warmth into our persons.

The same exercise can be used for cooling. Or,
by visualizing, in place of the tube, a sailor's knot
being untied on the screen of your mind, it is often
possible to eliminate the muscular spasm that follows a sharp, superficial blow. What is happening in
each of these exercises is that the power of visualiza-
tion (mental imagery) is being applied to the pattern
of breathing (physical respiration) for the purpose of
continued functioning in unfavorable circumstances.

The Energizing Breath: Here is an exercise given by
David Sobel and Faith Hornbacher in their useful
book, *To Your Health.* As the authors point out, the
technique is one yogis call "skull shining," because
of the sensation of radiant brightness it brings to
your head. While standing or sitting, inhale deeply
through your *nose,* and press your lips close to your
teeth, leaving only a narrow slit between. Then ex-

hale forcefully through this slit in a series of short, distinct bursts of air. After exhaling all the air, take several relaxed breaths, and repeat once or twice more.

With this exercise, once again, the question of why you do it is vital. Is it to stay awake through a dull meeting, or to appear alert in a classroom? These might be among the short-range effects of the "skull-shining" exercise. But behind these will be the larger goal of referring the function of alert attention at any given moment—what we have identified as value-loaded time—back to the personal will. Otherwise the energy of that attention can be squandered at the level of the public and private self, in superficial activities that bring only transitory rewards. This is the paradox of "empty success."

The goal of breath-control exercises thus is not simply to make the body-machine more efficient, but the ability (1) to accommodate more readily to changes in external conditions; (2) to reinforce the experience of willing our response to those circumstances; (3) to increase sensory awareness of all parts of the body and their immediate surroundings; and (4) to help us attune our own personal rhythms to the rhythm and flux of the world around us.

10.
The Thriving
Person

"In the ten thousand years of human history ours is the first era in which man has become a problem to himself, in which he no longer knows what he is, and at the same time knows that he does not know it." Today, what Max Scheler wrote fifty years ago is truer than ever. Yet the notion of self-actualization, self-reliance, self-realization has recently come in for a good deal of criticism. Charges of "narcissism" and "self-worship" have been leveled at any system or theory that emphasizes self-awareness as a condition for healthy living. And no doubt there is something in these criticisms. We have seen how the Cultist tends to objectify "awareness," turning it into a commercial product. Throughout, the aim of this book has been toward keeping the way open to what lies beyond such false gods—the vision that was eloquently set forth by Walt Whitman, when he wrote in *Democratic Vistas:*

> There is, in sanest hours, a consciousness, a thought that rises, independent, lifted out from all else, calm, like the stars, shining eternal. This is the thought of identity,—yours for you, whoever you are, as mine for me. Miracle of miracles, beyond statement, most spiritual and vaguest of earth's dreams, yet hardest basic fact, and only entrance to all facts. In such devout hours, in the midst of the significant wonders of heaven and earth (significant only because of the Me in the center), creeds, conventions, fall away and become of no account before this simple idea. Under the luminousness of real vision, it alone takes possession, takes value.

Such, then, is the consciousness of the thriving person.

Other qualities that characterize the thriving person are these:

The thriving person is ACCEPTING. He accepts, first of all, his own uniqueness of temperament, his own unique body and mind. He understands that there is no one else in the world quite like himself, and that even he will never fully comprehend every aspect of his idiosyncratic nature. He accepts that what understanding he does achieve will come in continuing revelations of the needs and values that spring from his personal core. He is, therefore, almost continuously in vigilant dialogue with himself, and will set aside specific times to hear and heed the "inner impulse voices" of that true nature.

He may meditate in some formal way, reserving some time each day for the purpose. He may jog or run, go fishing, or sit silently in his room. Whatever mode he chooses, it will be in the spirit of accepting the messages of his personal nature. It is the intention, not the form, that is important. Devoting regular time to such inner listening leads the thriving person to another kind of accepting: to accepting the mission that will express in the world the uniqueness of his own nature. This mission may not be the clear mandate of God to St. Francis to rebuild the Church; but to him who hears, it will be as precious. His mission will call him to make his values come alive, to demonstrate outside himself what within himself he believes to be good. If he accepts the destiny he hears in "uncommon hours," he returns to the world around him with a clarity and energy that make his decisions more confident and more daring—and more likely to succeed. It is his personal nature that both reveals that vision, and accepts it as the agenda to which his private and public energies must be directed. The meditative attitude is reserved for that personal nature; it is a retreat to what we have called "the island of 'I'," the anchoring-point from which all the public and private voyages begin, and to which those journeys return. Acceptance, then, also involves the acknowledgment that the internal focus of the personal nature must be allowed to rule, must be the final tribunal for the resolution of conflicts, and the mastermind of strategies for coping with crisis.

The accepting person always appears to us to be comfortable in his skin, not self-conscious (in the adolescent sense), not needing confirmation of his own worth from others. He accepts those others, too, as one who loves easily, trusts widely, and remains open to newness, because he has no need to defend a shaky sense of who he is. Finally, the thriving person accepts that what he makes of his life is the result of choosing, choosing at every moment what he will do in the next, and accepting the results of those choices—even if they fail—because he also accepts his creative ability to make still other and better choices.

The thriving person is RESPONSIBLE. He can answer to himself and to others for how he behaves. On the personal side, he acknowledges honestly when he has failed to act in accord with his inner values: this can be for as petty a lapse as fibbing about how he liked the lima-bean casserole, or as serious a violation of self as signing a loyalty oath he believes to be wrong. On the private and public side, his responsibility is equally obligatory: he acknowledges openly that he will not please another simply to keep things "smooth"; conversely, he is obliged to express good feelings and love when he experiences them. In any event, the responsible style calls for a conscious taking into account—for oneself and for others—that not only acts, but also emotions and ideas have consequences, and that these consequences will not always be pleasant. An act or idea can almost always be *expressed* pleasantly; but the responsible person knows he may afterwards feel pain or loneliness as a result of what he has said or done.

The responsible person asks not only, "Should I call in sick today?" but also "Is this job the one that permits me the fullest expression of my talents and gifts?" He asks not only, "Can I help my wife by doing the dishes?" but also, "Am I helping her resolve her doubts about a career?"

The responsible person regards his circumstances as the raw material with which he can work to create a life he considers worthy. He remembers that, as Lewis Mumford has put it, "in the moral life, future intentions are more important than past causes." His responsibility is to that future vision, whether it be in the next moment, when he has a choice between lying or telling the truth; or in the longer-range choice between staying in a dead-end career or risking the move to a new one.

The thriving person is CREATIVE. He recognizes that the smallest act as well as the grandest gesture can reflect his ideas of beauty and form. He bakes a loaf of bread with the same care he gives to designing a house. He knows himself to have productive energy that goes beyond his survival needs; and he knows he can choose the substance and style of his creations. He acquires greater skill at his work not simply to make the job easier, but to free himself for new and tougher jobs.

Whereas most of us fear that "creativity" expresses itself only in the special gifts of a Mozart or a Rembrandt, the thriving person is one who is continually uncovering and accepting the form his creativity will take. The creation of such a person may be a friendship, or the care of a child, or advice to someone in distress. But whatever he does, for the thriving person, as for any artist, to be creative is a deep, personal need. For such a person, creativity is not a defense, not simply a way to make the best of an unpleasant situation. Rather, the creative process continually involves personal values and beliefs, always with the hope of perhaps contributing something not only new but lasting to the world we live in.

The thriving person is DEVOTED. The commitment he makes—to his creative projects, to other persons, to the world at large—takes on the tone of dedication. The thriving person, having heard his vocation, commits whatever resources he has to what he does, in the conviction that it is worth effort, risk, even perhaps his life.

Devotion has always implied a religious commitment, a way of worship. What the thriving person teaches us is that the energy of devotion can equally be applied to well-defined personal beliefs, and acted upon with creative energy. This is what William Blake must have meant when he wrote, "Thou art a man, God is no more; thine own humanity learn to adore."

The thriving person is TRANSCENDING: that is, he finds an identity in himself with a natural world that lies beyond human society, and with a cosmos beyond either. At the deepest level of his consciousness, he transcends all immediate situation. He finds a relation to existence, as Kurt Goldstein put it, "in terms of the possible as well as the actual."

He can transcend time and space; able at times to see himself under the aspect of eternity, he ceases, for example, to be a scholar alone with his books, but becomes part of the endless procession of scholars who have gone before, and also those who will follow. He finds a relation to heroes, and to dead members of his family, through the contemplation of ideas and values he shares with them. He transcends his own class, his own past, and his own culture, finding an identity not simply with his country or his particular ethnic heritage, but with the human species as a whole. The thriving person is a citizen of the world—even, at moments, a citizen of all worlds.

Of those experiences with which we are all familiar—of losing ourselves in concentration, getting high on listening to music under the stars, or forgetting where we are at the sight of something beautiful —the thriving person has more than the rest of us. He does not shrink from these moments of transcendance, nor does he strive to experience them for the sake of the experience; but his life is in fact so designed as to favor their recurrence.

Above all, the thriving person is one whose life is MEANINGFUL. His life adds up to more than that he "made the best of it." Struggle and even failure become tolerable for him, so long as the effort he makes is consistent with the meaning he has discovered. He does not think only of leaving behind some legacy or monument that will survive him, but rather of maintaining allegiance to his own principles, of taking risks in the name of those principles, and of experiencing meaning not as a historical verdict but from day to day. The most mundane decisions bear on the larger sense of meaning. The thriving person follows the vigilant course urged by Emerson when he wrote: "Nothing can bring you peace but yourself; nothing can bring you peace but the triumph of principles."

The thriving person is, finally, one who lives COURAGEOUSLY. For such a person, courage is what Paul Tillich described as "that ethical act in which man affirms his own being in spite of those elements of his existence which conflict with his essential self-affirmation." Those "elements which conflict" may be inner as well as outer, as such a person well knows. What characterizes him is the ability to name and acknowledge such forces, and to emerge from the confrontation saying, "I believe in myself." It is the repeated affirmation of self-reliance in the face of such forces—both inner and outer—that enables the thriving person to continue on the path he has chosen. He sees clearly that no fixed end-point can be named and set up as the final goal; but because he has courage, he finds meaning in the journey itself.

To be able to ask questions to which there may be no answers—such is the courage of the thriving person. So it was that Rilke wrote to his young friend: ". . . be patient toward all that is unsolved in your heart and try to love the *questions themselves* like locked rooms and like books that are written in a very foreign tongue . . . The point is, to live everything. *Live* the questions now."

Acknowledgments

Until I finished writing this book I had not realized how much it is an attempt to flesh out, in modern terms, the major themes of Emerson's classic essay on "Self-Reliance." His voice has been a stimulus and a guide for me, his ideas an article of faith I shall always find inspiring.

The line going back into history from Emerson through Pico della Mirandola to Plato seems to me the richest intellectual heritage we have; likewise, the line forward from Emerson through William James, José Ortega y Gasset, and Lewis Mumford, up to the work of Abraham Maslow, has had the most important impact on the way I think and live.

In particular, I was blessed in knowing Maslow, and his wife Bertha, and I was involved with several of his books during my career as an editor and publisher. His tutorial influence and friendship has made an incalculable impression on my life and thought. He was a philosopher of science, and a prophet for all of us who follow him in the study of human nature. I hope that those who share my respect for Maslow's energy and ideas will see in my work something of his affirmation and optimism.

I met Maslow in 1966 through a mutual friend, Henry Geiger, a man Abe once described, in what for him was unreserved praise, as the "only small-*p* philosopher alive in America, a man whose ideas will outlive those of better-known people by hundreds of years." For some years before meeting Maslow I had been making regular pilgrimages to visit Geiger. He is a man who treasures anonymity and privacy, but it was and is he who has been my best teacher—teacher not in the sense of one who fills you with "facts," but as a person who creates an atmosphere in which you can learn what is most important to yourself. Call them "guides," or, as Carl Rogers would have it, "facilitators," the effect of great men like Geiger is to enable us who know them to become vigorous and persistent learners.

In every one of Abraham Maslow's books he made special mention of the weekly journal, *Manas*, always listing its address, P. O. Box 32112, El Sereno Station, Los Angeles, California, 90032, and pointing out to his readers that *Manas* "applies [my] point of view to the personal and social philosophy of the intelligent layman." I share Maslow's admiration for *Manas*, and repeat his commendation of it, having read it unfailingly and with great reward every week since 1962, and having once published in book form an anthology of writings from it.

Just as those familiar with Abraham Maslow's ideas will have seen my debt to him in this book, so those who know anything about Psychosynthesis will recognize some familiar principles. Psychosynthesis is an educational and psychological system developed over a sixty-year period by the late Italian psychiatrist, Dr. Roberto Assagioli, whose work is now being carried on in the United States and Canada at two Institutes, one in San Francisco, the other in Montreal. I have had training in Psychosynthesis, and I want to express openly and gratefully my debt to Assagioli's ideas, and to those who are extending them. (A journal, *Synthesis,* is published from 3352 Sacramento St., San Francisco, California 94118 for those interested in exploring this comprehensive approach to the task of personal growth.

To many others I am indebted for direct and indirect help during the writing of this book: Rabbi Leonard Beerman; Jeanne Bornstein; Dr. Jo Boufford; Dr. Robert B. Greifinger; Al Chung-liang Huang; Michael and Ann Loeb; Stuart Miller; Michael and Dulce Murphy; Alan Ravage; Leni Schwartz; Samuel S. Vaughan; Bill Whitehead; Dr. Harold B. Wise; and the Benjamin Rosenthal Foundation, which supported projects on which Leni Schwartz, Harold Wise, and I worked together. A number of the ideas in this book stemmed from that stimulating connection.

For specific and continuing help with the manuscript itself, my special thanks go to Cecilia Hunt of Bantam Books and Jack Macrae of E. P. Dutton. They have helped make my move from the editor's to the author's side of the desk, if not quite painless, at least possible, and their comments and suggestions helped me immensely.

Finally, neither the six small letters that spell out the dedication of this book, nor even this longer sentence can possibly acknowledge appropriately the endless acts of love, guidance, and rescue performed by my wife, Ann Arensberg. My debt to her crowns all others.

Salisbury, Connecticut
November, 1977

Recommended Readings

ALEXANDER, F. M. *The Resurrection of the Body.* New York: Delta Books, 1969.

ALLPORT, GORDON W. *Becoming.* New Haven: Yale University Press, 1955.

_____*Pattern and Growth in Personality.* New York: Holt, Rinehart and Winston, 1961.

ANGYAL, ANDRAS. *Foundations for a Science of Personality.* New York: Viking Press, 1972.

_____*Neurosis and Treatment.* New York: Viking Press, 1973.

ASSAGIOLI, ROBERTO. *Psychosynthesis.* New York: Viking Press, 1971.

_____*The Act of Will.* New York: Penguin, 1972.

AUROBINDO, SRI. *The Mind of Light.* New York: E. P. Dutton, 1971.

_____*The Future Evolution of Man.* New York: Humanities Press, 1971.

_____*The Life Divine.* New York: India Library Society, 1965.

BENNETT, ARNOLD. *How To Live On 24 Hours A Day.* New York: Cornerstone Library, 1962.

BINSWANGER, LEOPOLD. *Being-in-the-World,* ed. by J. Needleman. New York: Harper & Row, 1963.

BLOFELD, JOHN. *I Ching: The Book of Change.* New York: E. P. Dutton, 1966.

BOSS, MEDARD. *Psychoanalysis and Daseinanalysis.* New York: Basic Books, 1963.

BRONOWSKI, JACOB. *Science and Human Values.* New York: Harper & Row, 1972.

BUBER, MARTIN. *I and Thou.* New York: Scribner, 1970.

_____*Between Man and Man.* New York: Macmillan, 1965.

CAMUS, ALBERT. *The Myth of Sisyphus.* New York: Knopf, 1955.

_____*The Plague.* New York: Modern Library, 1948.

CARLSON, RICK J. *The End of Medicine.* New York: Wiley, 1974.

CUSHMAN, ROBERT. *Therapeia.* Chapel Hill, North Carolina: University of North Carolina Press, 1958.

DELLA MIRANDOLA, GIOVANNI PICO. *Oration on the Dignity of Man.* Chicago: Henry Regnery, 1956.

DUBOS, RENE. *Man Adapting.* New Haven: Yale University Press, 1965.

EMERSON, RALPH WALDO. *Essays.* New York: E. P. Dutton, 1972.

_____*Selected Writings.* New York: Modern Library, 1950.

ERIKSON, ERIK. *Childhood and Society.* New York: W. W. Norton, 1964.

_____*Identity and the Life Cycle.* International University Press, 1967.

FELDENKRAIS, MOSHE. *Awareness Through Movement.* New York: Harper & Row, 1972.

FRANK, JEROME. *Persuasion and Healing.* New York: Schocken Books, 1975.

FRANKL, VIKTOR. *Man's Search for Meaning.* New York: Pocket Books, 1970.

_____*Man for Himself.* New York: Fawcett, 1968.

_____*The Doctor and the Soul.* New York: Vintage, 1973.

FROMM, ERICH. *Escape from Freedom.* New York: Avon, 1969.

_____*The Art of Loving.* New York: Bantam, 1970.

GALDSTON, IAGO. *Psychiatry and the Human Condition.* New York: Brunner Mazel, 1977.

GOLDSTEIN, KURT. *Human Nature in the Light of Psychopathology.* New York: Schocken Books, 1963.

GREEN, ELMER, and ALYCE GREEN. *Beyond Biofeedback.* New York: Delacorte Seymour Lawrence, 1977.

HORNEY, KAREN. *Self Analysis.* New York: W. W. Norton, 1942.

_____ *Neurosis and Human Growth.* New York: W. W. Norton, 1950.

HUANG, AL CHUNG-LIANG. *Embrace Tiger, Return to Mountain.* Lafayette, California: Real People Press, 1972.

Human Nature (periodical), 757 Third Avenue, New York City 10017.

HUIZINGA, JOHAN. *Homo Ludens.* Boston: Beacon Press, 1955.

HUXLEY, ALDOUS. *The Perennial Philosophy.* New York: Harper & Row, 1945.

_____ *The Doors of Perception.* New York: Harper & Row, 1954.

HUXLEY, JULIAN, ed. *The Humanist Frame.* New York: Harper & Row, 1962.

JAMES, MURIEL, and DOROTHY JONGEWARD. *Born to Win.* Reading, Mass.: Addison–Wesley, 1971.

JAMES, WILLIAM. *The Principles of Psychology* (2 vols.). New York: Dover Publications, 1950.

_____ *The Varieties of Religious Experience.* New York: Collier Books, 1961.

JOURARD, SIDNEY. *The Transparent Self.* Princeton, N. J.: Van Nostrand, 2nd ed., 1971.

JUNG, C. G. *Modern Man in Search of a Soul.* New York: Harcourt, Brace, Jovanovich, 1968.

_____ *Psychological Reflections.* Princeton, N. J.: Princeton University Press, 1970.

_____ *Man and His Symbols.* New York: Dell, 1969.

_____ *The Undiscovered Self.* Boston: Atlantic Press, 1958.

KAHLER, ERICH. *The Tower and the Abyss.* New York: Viking Press, 1967.

KOHLER, WOLFGANG. *The Place of Value in a World of Facts.* New York: Liveright, 1938.

KRUTCH, JOSEPH WOOD. *The Measure of Man.* New York: Grosset & Dunlap, 1968.

_____ *Human Nature and the Human Condition.* New York: Random House, 1959.

KUVALAYANANDA, SWAMI, and DR. S. L. VINEKAR. *Yogic Therapy.* New Delhi Ministry of Health, 1971.

LAKEIN, ALAN. *How to Get Control of Your Time and Life.* New York: New American Library, 1974.

LEONARD, GEORGE. *The Ultimate Athlete.* New York: Dell, 1975.

LESHAN, LAWRENCE. *The Medium, the Mystic, and the Physicist.* New York: Ballantine, 1975.

_____ *How to Meditate.* New York: Bantam, 1975.

LUCE, GAY GAER. *Body Time.* New York: Bantam, 1973.

Manas (periodical) P.O. Box 32112, El Sereno Station, Los Angeles, California 90032.

MASLOW, ABRAHAM. *Toward a Psychology of Being.* Princeton, N. J.: Van Nostrand, 1968.

_____ *The Psychology of Science.* Chicago: Henry Regnery, 1969.

_____ *Motivation and Personality.* New York: Harper & Row, 1970.

_____ *Religions, Values and Peak Experiences.* New York: Viking Press, 1970.

_____ *The Farther Reaches of Human Nature.* New York: Viking Press, 1971.

_____ *Eupsychian Management.* Homewood, Ill.: Richard D. Irwin, 1965.

MASLOW, ABRAHAM (ed.) *New Knowledge in Human Values.* Chicago: Henry Regnery, 1959.

MASLOW, A., and HUNG-MIN CHIANG. *Healthy Personality.* Princeton, N. J.: Van Nostrand, 1969.

MATSON, FLOYD W. *The Broken Image.* New York: Doubleday, 1973.

MAY, ROLLO. *The Meaning of Anxiety.* New York: W. W. Norton, rev. ed., 1977.

_____ *Man's Search for Himself.* New York: Dell, 1973.

_____ *Love and Will.* New York: Dell, 1973.

MAY, ROLLO (ed.) *Existential Psychology.* New York: Random House, 1969.

MAY, ROLLO; ERNEST ANGEL; HENRI ELLENBERGER. *Existence.* New York: Simon & Schuster, 1973.

MEAD, MARGARET. *New Lives for Old.* New York: William Morrow, 1956.

MUMFORD, LEWIS. *The Conduct of Life.* New York: Harcourt, Brace, Jovanovich, 1960.

_____ *The Transformations of Man.* London: Allen & Unwin, 1957.

_____ *The Pentagon of Power.* New York: Harcourt, Brace, Jovanovich, 1970.

MURPHY, GARDNER. *Human Potentialities.* New York: Viking Press, 1975.

MURPHY, GARDNER, and LOIS MURPHY. *Asian Psychology.* New York: Harper & Row, 1968.

MURPHY, MICHAEL. *Golf in the Kingdom.* New York: Dell, 1974.

ORNSTEIN, ROBERT. *The Psychology of Consciousness.* New York: Pelican Books, 1975.

_____*The Nature of Human Consciousness.* San Francisco: W. H. Freeman, 1972.

ORTEGA Y GASSET, JOSE. *Man and Crisis.* New York: W. W. Norton, 1958.

_____*What Is Philosophy?* New York: W. W. Norton, 1960.

_____*The Revolt of the Masses.* New York: W. W. Norton, 1957.

PERLS, FREDERICK. *Gestalt Therapy Verbatim.* New York: Bantam Books, 1971.

POLANYI, MICHAEL. *The Tacit Dimension.* New York: Doubleday, 1967.

_____*Personal Knowledge.* New York: Harper & Row, 1964.

_____*The Study of Man.* Chicago: University of Chicago Press, 1970.

RICHARDS, M. C. *Centering.* Middletown, Conn.: Wesleyan University Press, 1964.

_____*The Crossing Point.* Middletown, Conn.: Wesleyan University Press, 1973.

RIESMAN, DAVID. *The Lonely Crowd.* New Haven, Conn.: Yale University Press, 1969.

RILKE, RAINER MARIA. *Letters to a Young Poet.* New York: W. W. Norton, 1962.

_____*Notebooks of Malte Laurids Brigge.* New York: W. W. Norton, 1964.

ROGERS, CARL. *Client-Centered Therapy.* Boston: Houghton Mifflin, 1951.

_____*On Becoming a Person.* Boston: Houghton Mifflin, 1961.

ROSS, NANCY WILSON. *Three Ways of Asian Wisdom.* New York: Simon & Schuster, 1966.

ROSZAK, THEODORE. *The Unfinished Animal.* New York: Harper & Row, 1975.

SMUTS, JAN C. *Holism and Evolution.* New York: Viking, 1961.

SOBEL, DAVID, and FAITH HORNBACHER. *To Your Health.* New York: Grossman, 1973.

SOBEL, DAVID. *Health and Healing: Ancient and Modern.* New York: Harcourt, Brace, Jovanovich, 1978.

Synthesis (periodical). 3352 Sacramento Street, San Francisco, California 94118.

TEILHARD DE CHARDIN, PIERRE. *The Future of Man.* New York: Harper & Row, 1967.

_____*The Phenomenon of Man.* New York: Harper & Row, 1959.

_____*Human Energy*. New York: Harcourt, Brace, Jovanovich, 1969.

THOREAU, HENRY DAVID. *Walden and Other Writings*. New York: Bantam, 1971.

TILLICH, PAUL. *The Courage to Be*. New Haven: Yale University Press, 1952.

WATTS, ALAN. *Psychotherapy East and West*. New York: Random House, 1973.

_____*Tao: The Watercourse Way*. New York: Pantheon, 1976.

WEIL, SIMONE. *The Need for Roots*. New York: Harper & Row, 1952.

WEISS, PAUL. *Man's Freedom*. New Haven: Yale University Press, 1950.

WELCH, HOLMES. *Taoism*. Boston: Beacon Press, 1957.

WHEELIS, ALLEN. *The Quest for Identity*. New York: W. W. Norton, 1958.

WHITMAN, WALT. *The Portable Walt Whitman*. New York: Viking Press, 1945.

ZIMMER, HENRY R. *Hindu Medicine*. Baltimore: Johns Hopkins University Press, 1948.

ZINNSSER, HANS. *As I Remember Him*. Boston: Little, Brown, 1964.

Index

148 · Index